CRIMINAL
INVESTIGATIONS

CHILD ABDUCTION AND KIDNAPPING

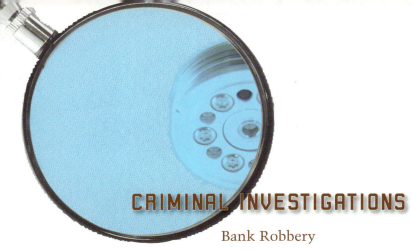

CRIMINAL INVESTIGATIONS

CRIMINAL
INVESTIGATIONS

CHILD ABDUCTION AND KIDNAPPING

SUSAN O'BRIEN

y

Consulting Editor: **JOHN L. FRENCH**,
Crime Scene Supervisor,
Baltimore Police Crime Laboratory

9/09

CHELSEA HOUSE
P U B L I S H E R S
An imprint of Infobase Publishing

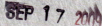

CRIMINAL INVESTIGATIONS: Child Abduction and Kidnapping

Chelsea House
An imprint of Infobase Publishing
132 West 31st Street
New York NY 10001

Library of Congress Cataloging-in-Publication Data
O'Brien, Susan.
Child abduction and kidnapping / Susan O'Brien, John L. French.
p. cm. — (Criminal investigations)
Includes bibliographical references and index.
ISBN-13: 978-0-7910-9403-7 (alk. paper)
ISBN-10: 0-7910-9403-0 (alk. paper)
1. Abduction—United States—Juvenile literature. 2. Kidnapping—
United States—Juvenile literature. 3. Criminal investigation—
United States—Juvenile literature. I. French, John L. II. Title.
   HV6574.U6O37 2008   364.15′40830973—dc22
      2007049944

Text design by Erika K. Arroyo
Cover design by Ben Peterson

Cover: Neighbors Kate Langland *(left)* and Kim Ujifsa leave the home of
the Smart family to go and post fliers of Elizabeth Smart in
Salt Lake City, Utah, on June 5, 2002.

Printed in the United States of America

Bang FOF 10 9 8 7 6 5 4 3 2 1

This book is printed on acid-free paper.

All links and Web addresses were checked and verified to be
correct at the time of publication. Because of the dynamic nature
of the Web, some addresses and links may have changed
since publication and may no longer be valid.

For my family, every child, and every protector

Special thanks to Sgt. James A. Koontz of the Loudoun County, Virginia, Sheriff's Office; Rick Woody of the Kacie Woody Foundation; and Liss Hart-Haviv of Take Root for their generous assistance

Contents

Foreword

In 2000 there were 15,000 murders in the United States. During that same year about a half million people were assaulted, 1.1 million cars were stolen, 400,000 robberies took place, and more than 2 million homes and businesses were broken into. All told, in the last year of the twentieth century, there were more than 11 million crimes committed in this country.*

In 2000 the population of the United States was approximately 280 million people. If each of the above crimes happened to a separate person, only 4 percent of the country would have been directly affected. Yet everyone is in some way affected by crime. Taxes pay patrolmen, detectives, and scientists to investigate it, lawyers and judges to prosecute it, and correctional officers to watch over those convicted of committing it. Crimes against businesses cause prices to rise as their owners pass on the cost of theft and security measures installed to prevent future losses. Tourism in cities, and the money it brings in, may rise and fall in part due to stories about crime in their streets. And every time someone is shot, stabbed, beaten, or assaulted, or when someone is jailed for having committed such a crime, not only they suffer but so may their friends, family, and loved ones. Crime affects everyone.

It is the job of the police to investigate crime with the purpose of putting the bad guys in jail and keeping them there, hoping thereby to punish past crimes and discourage new ones. To accomplish this a police officer has to be many things: dedicated, brave, smart, honest, and imaginative. Luck helps, but it's not required. And there's one more virtue that should be associated with law enforcement. A good police officer is patient.

Patience is a virtue in crime fighting because police officers and detectives know something that most criminals don't. It's not a secret, but most lawbreakers don't learn it until it is too late. Criminals who make money robbing people, breaking into houses, or stealing cars; who live by dealing drugs or committing murder; who spend their days on the wrong side of the law, or commit any other crimes, must remember this: a criminal has to get away with every crime he or she commits. However, to get criminals off the street and put them behind bars, the police only have to catch a criminal once.

The methods by which police catch criminals are varied. Some are as old as recorded history and others are so new that they have yet to be tested in court. One of the first stories in the Bible is of murder, when Cain killed his brother Abel (Genesis 4:1–16). With few suspects to consider and an omniscient detective, this was an easy crime to solve. However, much later in that same work, a young man named Daniel steps in when a woman is accused of an immoral act by two elders (Daniel 13:1–63). By using the standard police practice of separating the witnesses before questioning them, he is able to arrive at the truth of the matter.

From the time of the Bible to almost present day, police investigations did not progress much further than questioning witnesses and searching the crime scene for obvious clues as to a criminal's identity. It was not until the late 1800s that science began to be employed. In 1879 the French began to use physical measurements and later photography to identify repeat offenders. In the same year a Scottish missionary in Japan used a handprint found on a wall to exonerate a man accused of theft. In 1892 a bloody fingerprint led Argentine police to charge and convict a mother of killing her children, and by 1905 Scotland Yard had convicted several criminals thanks to this new science.

Progress continued. By the 1920s scientists were using blood analysis to determine if recovered stains were from the victim or suspect, and the new field of firearms examination helped link bullets to the guns that fired them.

Nowadays, things are even harder on criminals, when by leaving behind a speck of blood, dropping a sweat-stained hat, or even taking a sip from a can of soda, they can give the police everything they need to identify and arrest them.

In the first decade of the twenty-first century the main tools used by the police include

- questioning witnesses and suspects
- searching the crime scene for physical evidence
- employing informants and undercover agents
- investigating the whereabouts of previous offenders when a crime they've been known to commit has occurred
- using computer databases to match evidence found on one crime scene to that found on others or to previously arrested suspects
- sharing information with other law enforcement agencies via the Internet
- using modern communications to keep the public informed and enlist their aid in ongoing investigations

But just as they have many different tools with which to solve crime, so too do they have many different kinds of crime and criminals to investigate. There is murder, kidnapping, and bank robbery. There are financial crimes committed by con men who gain their victim's trust or computer experts who hack into computers. There are criminals who have formed themselves into gangs and those who are organized into national syndicates. And there are those who would kill as many people as possible, either for the thrill of taking a human life or in the horribly misguided belief that it will advance their cause.

The Criminal Investigations series looks at all of the above and more. Each book in the series takes one type of crime and gives the reader an overview of the history of the crime, the methods and motives behind it, the people who have committed it, and the means by which these people are caught and punished. In this series celebrity crimes will be discussed and exposed. Mysteries that have yet to be solved will be presented. Readers will discover the truth about murderers, serial killers, and bank robbers whose stories have become myths and legends. These books will explain how criminals can separate a person from his hard-earned cash, how they prey on the weak and helpless, what is being done to stop them, and what one can do to help prevent becoming a victim.

John L. French,
Crime Scene Supervisor,
Baltimore Police Crime Laboratory

* Federal Bureau of Investigation. "Uniform Crime Reports, Crime in the United States 2000." Available online. URL: http://www.fbi.gov/ucr/00cius.htm. Accessed January 11, 2008.

Introduction

According to the U.S Department of Justice, more than 250,000 children are abducted each year.[1] That is a startling number that raises a lot of questions. Who are these children? Who kidnaps them? Why are they taken? Most importantly, how can this problem be solved?

Kidnapping has attracted attention throughout history, right into the present, when some of the most popular television shows and books focus on abduction. It's a topic that evokes strong emotions and challenges people to face the worst and do their best.

One benefit of examining past cases—and learning how to investigate new ones—is empowerment. No job is more worthwhile than protecting children. That's why so many people make it their goal. From experts to volunteers to kids themselves, a dedicated force is working hard to prevent abduction and bring **victims** home. Understanding the history of abduction is a step in that direction.

THE EARLY HISTORY OF KIDNAPPING

The word **kidnap** is actually a combination of two terms, *kid* (**child**) and *nap* (seize). It dates back to the 1600s, when kidnappers stole children to work on colonial plantations. **Abduct**, which is often used interchangeably with *kidnap*, comes from the Latin prefix *ab* (away) and verb *ducere* (to lead).[2]

Long before kidnapping had its present name, however, it was part of the human experience. Ancient documents such as the Bible describe kidnappings of adults and children. In American history, kidnappings occurred during the struggle between the native population and settlers; enslavement of Africans was a massive form of abduction.

Over time, some of the most infamous U.S. abductions have involved children. These crimes have had a major influence on how individuals, communities, and investigators react to kidnapping. One of the first prominent examples had two victims, but only one safe return.

Charles and Walter Ross

*It was July 1, 1874, and four-year-old Charles Ross (known as Charley) was outside with his six-year-old brother Walter near Germantown, Pennsylvania. According to Walter, two familiar men were able to **lure** the boys into a carriage, offering to buy them firecrackers. While Walter was sent into a store to make purchases, Charley disappeared with the men, never to be seen again.*

*The family received a series of **ransom** notes, but no effort to find Charley worked, including offering a large reward. A tip eventually identified two men as his kidnappers, but they died after being shot during a burglary. Months later, Pennsylvania passed a law to help with the case, which changed kidnapping from a **misdemeanor** (a less serious crime) to a **felony** (a more serious crime) and gave one month of amnesty to anyone hiding a child.[3] That meant someone holding Charley could bring him forward without being punished. Sadly, no one did. Although an accomplice was convicted on conspiracy charges in the abduction and sent to prison, Charley's actual fate was never discovered.*

The kidnapping was called the crime of the century and America's first major ransom kidnapping.[4] It captured newspaper headlines and the hearts of the American people. The entire country was forced to contemplate how abductions should be handled.

The Lindbergh Baby

Charles Lindbergh, the first pilot to cross the Atlantic Ocean alone, was an American hero and a worldwide celebrity. Three years after his amazing flight, he and his wife, Anne, had a baby, Charles Augustus Lindbergh Jr. Baby Charles grew into a blond, blue-eyed 20 month old. But sometime

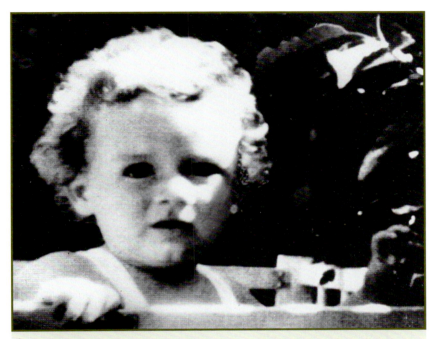

This is a 1932 photograph of Charles A. Lindbergh Jr. taken shortly before he was kidnapped from his parents' home on March 1. *AP*

after he was put to bed on the evening of March 1, 1932, he disappeared.

A search of the Lindbergh property near Hopewell, New Jersey, revealed clues such as footprints, a ladder near the nursery window, and a ransom note demanding $50,000. Once word got out, the family began receiving prank phone calls and new ransom demands.[5] Lindbergh arranged to pay the original ransom through a third party, but the baby was not returned.

A body identified as baby Charles was found two months later in woods several miles from the family mansion. It was clear that he had not survived long after being taken. The investigation continued with special focus on the ransom money. Officials knew the bills' serial numbers, and one of the bills was spent at a gas station. The customer was believed to be Bruno Hauptmann, a 35-year-old carpenter

HANDWRITING ANALYSIS

When an abductor writes a ransom note, handwriting analysis can help with the investigation. In the Lindbergh kidnapping, for instance, ransom notes were compared to writing samples from Bruno Hauptmann, who was convicted in the case. This is one of the most famous and debated examples of **forensic** handwriting analysis. Questions linger today as to the accuracy of the handwriting analysis, whether or not Hauptmann wrote the notes, and whether or not he was actually guilty. However, there is no question that the handwriting analysis presented during the trial played a part in convicting Hauptmann.

Document experts say every person's handwriting is unique. They notice features such as how writing is slanted, formed, and spaced, and how individual letters are formed, particularly those with loops or tails. But when investigators check a suspect's handwriting, they don't simply instruct the person to "write something." They follow guidelines, such as

- Use a writing instrument and kind of paper that matches the original document.
- Include some wording that appears in the initial document.
- Do not tell the subject how to spell or use punctuation.
- Have the individual write at least three copies.

What if suspects try to change their handwriting to disguise themselves? They still may leave telltale clues. For example, they might use similar words or make similar mistakes.

with a criminal record and a stash of the ransom money at his home.

Although Hauptmann was convicted in 1935 and executed for the crime in 1936, many people thought he was **framed**, and some claimed the whole story was false—that Charles never died. One woman said he was raised in her family, but **DNA** tests proved her wrong in 2000.[6]

In the wake of the Lindbergh baby kidnapping, the **Lindbergh Law** (also known as the Federal Kidnapping Act, 1932)

Samuel Small, New York professional writing expert, compares ransom notes from the Lindbergh kidnap case with the handwriting of Bruno Hauptmann, the main suspect in the kidnapping and murder of the 20-month-old infant. *AP*

*was passed, which authorized **federal** investigation of suspected interstate kidnappings.*

There are many similarities between the Ross and Lindbergh abductions. In both cases, there were ransom demands and attempts to negotiate with kidnappers. Both kidnappings were heavily covered by the **media** and called crimes of the century. The public was fascinated, devastated, and eager to help. Laws were even passed related to the abductions. Tragically, nothing saved either Charles, and sometimes people interfered in hurtful ways. But the nation's awareness of kidnapping—and dedication to stopping it—grew by leaps and bounds.

WHY ABDUCTION HAPPENS

Charley Ross and Charles Lindbergh may have been kidnapped for ransom, but children today are rarely targeted for money, probably because abduction has become such a high-risk crime. So if hundreds of thousands of children are abducted each year, and kidnappers rarely profit financially from their acts, why do so many children disappear?

A highly respected research project called the Second National Incidence Studies of Missing, Abducted, Runaway, and Thrownaway Children (**NISMART-2**) provides some answers. (Figures from NISMART-2 generally refer to research conducted in 1999.) According to NISMART-2, there are two main categories of child abduction: **family abduction** and **nonfamily abduction**. The major difference is that the abductor either is or isn't a member (or representative) of the child's family. In both kinds of abduction, there may be more than one abductor, and offenders can be juveniles.

Family abductions are often motivated by disagreements between parents, particularly about **custody**. Sometimes other relatives are involved, such as grandparents, aunts, or uncles. NISMART-2 suggests that more than 200,000 children a year are victims of family abduction.

Nonfamily abductions are less common—totaling 58,200 per year in NISMART-2—yet they receive more attention. There is a misconception that strangers are primarily responsible for these kidnappings, but more than half of victims are abducted by people they know, NISMART-2 indicates. In most nonfamily cases overall, the child is physically or sexually assaulted. Robbery and ransom are relatively infrequent factors. Kidnappers who take infants, in contrast, are more likely to be motivated by a desire to have a family. Sometimes children are abducted during other crimes, such as stealing a car.

Stereotypical kidnappings are an extremely dangerous type of nonfamily abduction. Estimated at 115 per year in NISMART-2,

♀ ABDUCTION TRUE OR FALSE

Time has taught many lessons about child abduction, but there is still plenty of confusion about the subject. Try to separate fact from fiction by responding *true* or *false* to the following statements.

1. *There has been a dramatic increase in stereotypical kidnappings.*

   False. NISMART studies were published in 1990 and 2002, and although they are difficult to compare, they don't show an increase in stereotypical kidnappings.[7]

2. *Most abduction cases are solved.*

   True. The vast majority of abducted children are returned home or located alive.[8]

3. *When a nonfamily member takes a child, the victim is often a teen girl.*

   True. Boys and girls of all ages are potential victims, but girls between 12 and 17 years old are at particular risk.[9]

4. *There is a 48-hour waiting period before law enforcement will search for a missing child.*

   False. Families should report suspected kidnappings immediately, because there is no "waiting period" before missing child investigations ought to begin.

5. *Biological mothers commit more family abductions than biological fathers.*

   False. In family abductions, biological fathers are more likely to be the kidnapper.[10]

6. *Strangers who kidnap children are most often male.*

   True. Research suggests the overwhelming majority of these **perpetrators** are male.[11]

7. *The FBI can only investigate a kidnapping if the victim is taken across state lines.*

   False. The FBI says it will start a kidnapping investigation "involving a missing child 'of tender years' even though there is no known interstate aspect. 'Tender years'

(continues)

(continued)

is generally defined as a child twelve years or younger. The FBI will monitor other kidnapping situations when there is no evidence of interstate travel, and it offers assistance from various entities including the FBI Laboratory."[12]

they are committed by strangers or slight acquaintances and involve a particularly serious element, such as ransom or loss of life. Victims of stereotypical kidnapping have a better chance of surviving than being killed, according to NISMART-2, but they are at much higher risk for death than other abducted children.

ABDUCTION AND KIDNAPPING TODAY

Society has taken a firm stand against abduction and kidnapping by making them crimes. A child (someone under the age of 18) is generally considered kidnapped when he or she is taken, detained, or hidden—such as by force, threat, trickery, or violence—in a way that is against the law.

This doesn't mean that if a custodial parent plans a surprise party for a child, tells the child to get in the car, and fibs about where they're going, an abduction is taking place. Nor does it mean that when police arrest a child, they are kidnappers. Abduction and kidnapping refer to situations in which something illegal happens.

The National Center for Missing & Exploited Children (**NCMEC**) lists many federal laws related to missing and abducted children. For example

■ The Uniform Child Custody Jurisdiction Act (1968) and the related Uniform Child Custody Jurisdiction and Enforcement Act (initiated in 1997) make it easier for states to cooperate and support each other in custody matters.

- The Parental Kidnapping Prevention Act (1980) encourages states to honor each other's child custody decisions when specific guidelines are met.
- The Missing Children Act (1982) authorizes federal collection and sharing of information that can help with various investigative tasks, including finding missing children.
- The Missing Children's Assistance Act (1984) requires the existence of a national missing children toll-free telephone line, help center, and clearinghouse (NCMEC).
- The National Child Search Assistance Act (1990) sets guidelines for reporting missing children. For example, law enforcement agencies must enter missing child cases into a Federal Bureau of Investigation (FBI) database called the National Crime Information Center (**NCIC**).
- The International Parental Kidnapping Crime Act (1993) defines how wrongfully taking a child away from the United States or retaining a child who is from the United States (in a non-U.S. location) can be a federal crime.
- The Jacob Wetterling Crimes Against Children and Sexually Violent Offender Registration Act (1994) calls for certain criminals to register information about themselves for 10 years.
- The Prosecutorial Remedies and Other Tools to end the Exploitation of Children Today Act of 2003 (PROTECT Act) strengthens reactions to abduction in many ways. For example, it makes kidnapping a more serious offense and improves the America's Missing: Broadcast Emergency Response Alert, or **AMBER Alert**, program, which informs and involves the public in some abduction cases.[13]

Kidnapping is taken seriously, and when children are abducted, it's comforting to know that an army of experts is available to find them. This book reveals how it's done. Just as importantly, it shows that everyone has a role to play in protecting children, including you.

Preliminary Investigation:
Asking Questions, Finding Answers

The morning of May 25, 1979, six-year-old Etan Patz left his New York apartment for school. His bus stop was nearby, and his mother stood watch as he walked away. It was his first time making the trip alone.

That afternoon, Etan did not return from school. Police arrived at his apartment around 5:30 p.m. and decided that neither young Etan nor his loving parents seemed responsible for his disappearance. **Polygraph** tests supported this belief, and a witness said the boy had never reached the bus.

That left daunting questions to be answered. Who had taken him—and why? In a city as crowded as New York, where could he be?

Etan's case was the top priority for the New York Police Department. They searched the area repeatedly and followed countless leads from the public, which had been flooded with news reports about him.

At first, Etan's mother believed someone childless and desperate to become a parent had taken her friendly, handsome child.[1] Over time, however, awareness grew about other possible motives, including sexual assault.

Julie Patz, mother of Etan Patz, speaking on NBC's *Today* show in New York City on March 26, 1981. *AP*

Years of investigation did not solve the mystery of Etan's disappearance. Yet its anniversary offers hope. In 1983 President Ronald Reagan declared May 25 National Missing Children's Day. This is a yearly opportunity to honor Etan and other children like him—and recommit the country to helping them.

Every abduction is unique, but Etan's case provides several examples of common steps in kidnapping investigations, such as interviewing family members and possible witnesses, conducting searches, following leads, and working with the media. It also illustrates how times have changed.[2] When Etan disappeared, investigators did not have the resources and technologies they have today. Now when a child is kidnapped, there is an organized response on a national level.

ON THE SCENE

Picture this: You're a newspaper reporter, and your editor assigns you a developing story. The president's airplane, Air Force One, has landed unexpectedly at the local airport, and you have to find out why.

En route to the scene, your mind and body are in high gear. You want to get there as quickly as possible, interview everyone involved, and see things for yourself. You start planning what to ask. Should you assume this is just a brief stop—no big deal? No, you decide. You'll treat the story seriously until the facts are in.

Being an investigator is similar to being a reporter. When a child is missing, it's important to arrive quickly, be prepared, and consider the potential gravity of the situation. According to NCMEC, "Assume that the child is in danger until the facts contradict that assumption."[3] An investigator who is too relaxed may miss chances to save a life. Other common advice for on-the-scene investigators is to cover the following issues:

- *What happened?* Interview people who may have helpful information. Talk with them separately so they don't influence each other's stories.

Police officers look over an area in Quartz Hill, California, where two teenage girls were abducted. Speedy arrival and thorough analysis of the scene are essential to the recovery of an abducted child. *Gene Breckner/AP*

- *What is the child like?* Obtain a complete physical and mental description. Review appearance, routines, abilities, and emotions.
- *Where could the child be?* Conduct a thorough search. For example, has the child simply hidden somewhere in or near the home?
- *Who has custody of the child?* Check to see if there are any disputes about this.
- *What do you notice about the child's environment?* Record any signs of abduction or other possibilities, such as running away.
- *What evidence can be protected?* Do not disturb possible clues about abductors or the child, such as fingerprints, footprints, and sources of DNA.
- *Who can provide photos or video of the child?* Request recent, high-quality color images.
- *What do people suspect happened to the child?* Investigators should ask others—and themselves—about this.
- *What is known about abduction in general?* Remember the major categories (family, nonfamily, and nonfamily stereotypical) and keep an open mind.

BEHIND THE SCENES

Return to the scenario in which you're reporting on the president. How could coworkers back at the newspaper office help? You'd want them to dig up as much relevant information as possible. You'd also ask them to verify things you learn on the scene so your article is accurate and complete. Meanwhile, they might post an initial headline on the paper's Web site: "President Arrives at Local Airport; More Information to Follow."

In the same way, officers who respond to missing child calls aren't working alone. Rather, if an abduction is suspected, they have local, state, and federal resources on their side. As a team, several agencies can investigate and publicize the case immediately. Helpers behind the scenes might

- Notify the entire law enforcement community so everyone can be on the lookout for the child and the abductor or abductors.
- Contact other sources of support, such as the **FBI**, NCMEC, NCIC, and state missing children's clearinghouses.
- Arrange for the use of tracking dogs, search volunteers, and other resources.
- Conduct background checks on those involved. For example, does anyone have a criminal record?
- See if there have been previous calls to the home about family problems or other concerns.
- Evaluate other calls in the area. Pay close attention to similar or strange occurrences.
- Keep collecting, organizing, and using information, leads, and evidence.
- Publicize the case through the media, fliers, AMBER Alerts, and other means of gaining the public's help.
- Research local sex offenders—people who have been convicted of certain particularly severe crimes.

THE FBI

Title 18 of the United States Code gives the FBI authority to investigate kidnappings. When a child is abducted and in danger, there is a special urgency to this mission. The FBI's Crimes Against Children Program may

- join the investigation
- examine areas for evidence
- send evidence to FBI labs
- create profiles of offenders
- help with large numbers of leads
- provide research about child abductions
- plan for a trial
- offer expert testimony[4]

♀ HUMAN TRAFFICKING

Summarized in a word, **human trafficking** is slavery. It's a crime often associated with other countries, but it happens in the United States too. Sometimes people are brought into the United States (often believing they are coming to a better life) and then exploited for sex or labor. Other times Americans are exploited for the same purposes. The U.S. Department of State says more than 50 percent of victims trafficked across international borders worldwide are children,[5] and the FBI estimates that more than 100,000 children and teens are trafficked in the United States today.[6]

According to the federal government, human traffickers may use kidnapping, assault, threats, control of money, and other means to enslave people.[7] In many cases, victims do not speak English, are hidden, and have been tricked into believing that if they get help, terrible things will happen. A psychological reaction called **Stockholm syndrome** may also influence them to protect their captors. Investigators must work hard to help fearful, deceived victims trust them.[8]

The passage of the Trafficking Victims Protection Act (TVPA) in 2000 was a big step toward helping victims and bringing traffickers to justice. But word still needs to spread about this crime. In 2006, the television show *Primetime Live* reported on American teens who said they were lured and abducted out of everyday life into sexual slavery.[9] Their stories showed the public that human trafficking is a worldwide crime that must be fought at home. Anyone with concerns about human trafficking can call the Trafficking Information and Referral Hotline at 1-888-373-7888.

These are just a few of the ways the FBI can help. Because investigators must react quickly to child kidnappings—especially nonfamily abductions—the FBI has created Child Abduction Rapid Deployment (**CARD**) teams. These groups are particularly knowledgeable, trained, and experienced, and they're ready to respond immediately to cases in any part of the country.

THE POLYGRAPH

It is common for investigators to use a polygraph—also known as a lie detector—to measure how someone's body reacts during an interview with a specialist. For example, how do the person's heart, skin, and breathing respond to various questions?

The polygraph has a long and controversial history. In 1923 it was ruled that a deception test was not admissible in court or generally accepted. More than a decade later in 1935, Bruno Hauptmann was tried in the infamous Lindbergh kidnapping case. He asked to take a lie detector test but was not allowed to proceed.[10] He was found guilty and put to death. Since then, there have been countless debates about if, when, and how the polygraph should be used.

Although scientific questions remain about the polygraph, today it is generally considered a valuable instrument, and some courts admit its results. Investigators use the polygraph to help solve abductions and other crimes.

After a kidnapping, for instance, potential suspects may take a polygraph test. If someone's test shows no deception, investigators might focus more on other people. That can be a huge relief to family members, who are often investigated first. On the other hand, if someone's examination shows deception or is inconclusive, investigators might look more closely at that person. Sometimes people even confess during a polygraph test.

SEX OFFENDERS

On the evening of July 29, 1994, seven-year-old Megan Kanka was near her home in Hamilton Township, New Jersey. That's when a neighbor who lived across the street, 33-year-old Jesse Timmendequas, lured her inside to see a puppy.

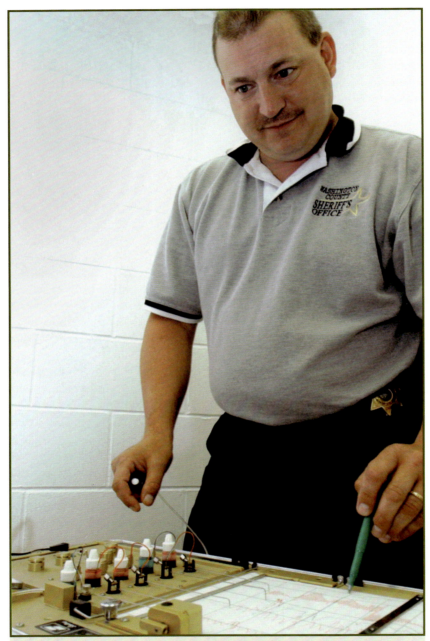

This investigator marks questions on the readout of a polygraph test. *Mike Buckley/AP*

Megan was not seen again until police became suspicious of Timmendequas—a convicted sex offender who had attacked children before—and he not only confessed, but led officials to Megan's body, which he had dumped in a park. She had been physically and sexually assaulted and murdered.

Learning about Timmendequas' criminal history (along with the records of his two roommates, who were also sex offenders) was helpful but maddening. What if neighbors had known about it earlier? Could this crime have been prevented?

Megan's family wanted states to notify residents about sex offenders. That goal became a reality when **Megan's Law** was passed in New Jersey in 1994—and then nationally in 1996. The law is part of the Jacob Wetterling Crimes Against Children and Sexually Violent Offender Registration Act (1994), which calls for certain criminals to register information about themselves so officials can keep better track of them.

A woman places flowers at a memorial site in Megan's Place, a small park built on the site where Megan Kanka was murdered. *Allen Oliver/ AP*

Laura Ahearn, executive director of Parents for Megan's Law, stands outside her children's courtroom on Long Island, New York. All 50 states have similar laws designed to inform communities about the presence of sex offenders. *Ed Bailey/AP*

Sex offender laws are controversial for many reasons, including their effects on offenders' privacy. Some critics worry that people will rely too much on notification and sex offender registries. Families must remember that many sex offenders aren't on lists or even caught. There is widespread support for sex offender laws, though, because sex offenses are so extreme, and protecting children is so important. Today, registries are available online as one form of notification.

A continued push for sex offender legislation resulted in the Adam Walsh Child Protection and Safety Act of 2006, named after a six-year-old boy who was abducted and killed in 1981. This law protects children in a variety of ways, including the use of a national public sex offender registry designed to provide a more accurate picture of sex offenders nationwide. Registries address concerns about individual offenders, such as, "Where do they live?" "Where do they work?" and "What do they look like?"

STEREOTYPICAL KIDNAPPING

When someone says the word *kidnapping*, what comes to mind? For many people, it's *stereotypical kidnapping*, which NISMART-2 defines as a nonfamily abduction in which

- the perpetrator is a stranger or slight acquaintance of the child and
- the child is kept overnight or
- the child is moved at least 50 miles or
- the child is held for ransom or
- the perpetrator plans to keep the child permanently or
- the child is killed.[11]

Stereotypical kidnappings are so shocking that they receive lots of news coverage. Some cases are followed intensely by the national media for long periods. All this attention can give the wrong impression that stereotypical kidnappings are common. But NISMART-2 shows they're rare—about 115 per year.

Yet media attention helps because investigators need information from the public, especially after suspected stereotypical kidnappings. That's because NISMART-2 shows that in 40 percent of these kidnappings, the child is killed—a huge number compared to nonfamily abductions overall, which 99 percent of children survive. Here's another disturbing, yet key, statistic: 74 percent of abducted children who are murdered die within the *first three hours* of their abduction.[12] So the more efficiently investigators work, the better.

NISMART-2 also shows that in stereotypical kidnappings, the child is often assaulted in some way and sometimes robbed, but ransom is hardly ever demanded. The most common victims are 12 and older (more girls than boys), and the most frequent abductors are under age 40 and male.

CLOSING CASES

Kidnapping is an upsetting topic. Remember that stereotypical kidnappings, even if they're all over the news, are rare. Kidnappings are usually *solved*. Children almost always return home.

Let's revisit the fictional president's landing one more time. It turns out he is ill and needs immediate medical attention. You don't know how things will unfold, but you're on top of the story. Every piece of information will be evaluated with your coworkers' help.

Just like a newspaper staff handling the story of a lifetime, a nationwide network is dedicated to solving abduction cases, and this network is bigger and stronger than ever before.

The AMBER Alert:
Communities on the Case

January 13, 1996, seemed like an ordinary day in Arlington, Texas. Nine-year-old Amber Hagerman had eaten at Burger King, shopped with her grandmother, and started a short bicycle ride around the block.[1] Then a witness heard her scream and saw a man force her into a black pickup truck. Even with a description of the crime, police could not find Amber or the man. Her lifeless body was found four days later in a ditch.

Although Amber's case was covered by TV and radio stations, people desperately wished more could have been done to help. What if citizens had been told right away about the abduction? Would that have made a difference?

No one should have to ask questions like these today. Amber's case remains unsolved, yet in others like it, AMBER Alerts are used to gain the public's assistance. Amber's life was taken. But the memory of it is still saving lives.

WHAT IS AN AMBER ALERT?

When severe weather such as a tornado threatens public safety, broadcasters use the Emergency Alert System (EAS) to warn people. The America's Missing: Broadcast Emergency Response (AMBER) Alert works in a similar way. In certain child abduction cases, law

Glenda Whitson holds a picture and flyers of her granddaughter, Amber Hagerman. Amber was abducted two blocks from Whitson's home while riding her bicycle. *Bill Janscha/AP*

enforcement shares information with broadcasting and transportation agencies. Then people watching TV, listening to the radio, or passing highway alert signs are given details that could rescue a child and stop a criminal. Some even ask to receive alerts by email or text message. AMBER Alerts can change and improve as technology develops. Already, they add thousands (or even millions) of volunteers to a case, all in an instant.

WHEN ARE AMBER ALERTS USED?

Imagine a neighbor's alarm system blaring unexpectedly. At first it would worry people. They might even call the police. But after a string of false alarms, they would start to ignore it—or at least wonder if it worked.

That's what could happen if AMBER Alerts were used every time a child disappears. Unfortunately, there are so many missing children that if AMBER Alerts were always activated, they would lose their impact. Officials would risk losing people's attention and confidence.

So how does law enforcement know when to issue an AMBER Alert? The U.S. Department of Justice offers some guidelines:

1. Use your best judgment to decide whether an abduction happened. Remember that stranger abductions are the most dangerous.
2. Think about the risk of injury or death. AMBER Alerts are important when a child might be seriously hurt.
3. Review what information is available. For example, can the victim, suspect, or vehicle be described to the public?
4. Consider the child's age. Rules are not the same in every state, but children 17 and younger may qualify for an AMBER Alert.
5. Enter abduction information into NCIC properly. This database helps officials keep track of cases nationwide.[2]

WHAT IF A CASE DOESN'T MEET AMBER ALERT GUIDELINES?

The Department of Justice recognizes that missing children cases deserve special attention, whether or not they qualify for an

A highway sign in Rocky Hill, Connecticut, flashes the state's first Amber Alert. *Bob Child/AP*

AMBER Alert. For this reason, it supports the Child Abduction Response Team (**CART**) program.

CARTs are made up of local professionals (including law enforcement) who participate in training about abduction issues and respond quickly when a child is missing. Since these groups are regional, each area can develop a team that meets its specific needs.

The CART program and the AMBER Alert system complement one another.

HOW WAS THE AMBER SYSTEM DEVELOPED?

The first AMBER Alert system was actually called the AMBER Plan. It was inspired by members of Amber Hagerman's commu-

♀ WHAT DO PEOPLE SAY ABOUT THE AMBER ALERT?

"Amber has always been a little mommy to small children, so this is just another way for her to help...She's keeping them safe."[3]

—Donna Norris, Amber Hagerman's mother

"My Administration is committed to continuing to expand, enhance, and coordinate the successful AMBER Alert system across America."

—President George W. Bush, 2004[4]

"If only we had the AMBER Plan when our son, Adam, was abducted, it may have saved his life."

—John and Revé Walsh, National Center for Missing & Exploited Children[5]

"The AMBER Plan is one more life saving tool to help recover abducted children when time is the enemy."

—Ernie Allen, President and CEO, National Center for Missing & Exploited Children[6]

nity, who were so affected by her abduction that they suggested the idea of radio alerts in future cases. Representatives of law enforcement and the media were receptive, and the AMBER Plan was born in 1996. Since then, its popularity has spread across the country. All 50 states use AMBER Alerts—not because they have to (participation is voluntary), but because they know the power of this investigative tool.

WHO HAS BEEN HELPED BY THE AMBER ALERT?

According to NCMEC's *AMBER Alert* guide, the first AMBER Plan success story involved a tiny victim: a two-month-old girl in the

Dallas/Fort Worth area. NCMEC says that on November 19, 1999, the infant's babysitter, Sandra Fallis, was expected to return the baby by 6:30 p.m. When they were significantly late, police were called, and there was a decision to make. Should the AMBER Plan be used? Was the baby in serious danger?

"A CHILD IS MISSING" ALERT

An additional alert is used in some parts of the United States with help from A Child Is Missing (**ACIM**), a nonprofit organization founded in 1997. ACIM notifies area residents and businesses by telephone about missing people—including children, the elderly, and the disabled—and encourages the public to join searches. The service is provided to law enforcement free of charge. According to ACIM, it works like this:

1. A child, elderly person, or disabled individual is reported missing.
2. Law enforcement calls ACIM.
3. ACIM collects details about the situation, including a description of the missing person.
4. ACIM determines how to keep in touch with law enforcement on the scene.
5. A recorded message is created with information for residents and businesses.
6. The place where the missing person was last seen is entered into a computer.
7. A database lists homes and businesses to be called.
8. People are alerted by phone with the recorded message.
9. If a child is reported missing near water, the calling area may be expanded over time.
10. ACIM communicates with law enforcement until the situation is resolved.
11. Paperwork is completed about what happened.[7]

ACIM says it can initiate 1,000 calls in 60 seconds and that it has helped to recover many people. ACIM maintains a list of success stories on its Web site (http://www.achildismissing.org).[8] The development of this program is something to watch closely.

A background check on Fallis revealed problems with drugs and driving. Because of what they learned, the police decided to issue an alert, complete with a description of Fallis's truck and license plate number. That made all the difference. Less than 30 minutes after the first alert, a man called 911 with exciting information. Fallis's vehicle was right in front of his. "That's her, I can't believe it!" he said. Police pulled over the truck, recovered the girl safely, and arrested Fallis, who was sentenced to 10 years' probation for the kidnapping.[9]

Older children were the subjects of another memorable alert years later. In the summer of 2002, two California girls, ages 17 and 16, were kidnapped at gunpoint and assaulted. The state's first AMBER Alert was used, and drivers took notice. They spotted the vehicle in question and contacted authorities, who fatally shot the suspect before rescuing the teens.

Los Angeles County Assistant Sheriff Larry Waldie was thrilled with the alert's impact, calling it "phenomenal" on CNN.[10] Another official believed that if more time had passed, the kidnapper would have murdered the victims.[11] The case was later credited with motivating other states to use AMBER Alerts.[12]

These are just two examples of how the AMBER Alert works. NCMEC has recorded more than 300 AMBER Alert successes[13], and that number will surely grow.

WHY ARE AMBER ALERTS SO IMPORTANT?

According to U.S. Department of Justice research, 74 percent of kidnapped children who were murdered died within the first three hours of their abduction.[14] Victims need to be found as soon as possible. Thankfully, AMBER Alerts are designed with this goal in mind.

But that isn't the only reason AMBER Alerts are trusted. In some cases, kidnappers actually hear AMBER Alerts and release children. For example, NCMEC documented a 2006 Minneapolis, Minnesota, case in which a woman took a car—with a toddler in the back seat—from outside a store. The father had left the engine running while he went inside. The suspect heard the alert on the radio, parked the vehicle in a lot, and fled without the child. The

Ten years after Amber Hagerman was kidnapped and murdered, the United States Postal Service issued this stamp in honor of the child recovery system that bears her name. *AP*

woman was later caught.[15] It is hoped that the success of AMBER Alerts will convince some would-be abductors to give up their plots before even taking a child.

In 2003 the PROTECT Act was passed. It has many provisions that help missing children, such as support for the AMBER Alert, including a national coordinator for the system. It's reassuring that what started in Texas has become a national priority—and proof that when a child is abducted, everyone can help.

Family Abduction:
Surprising Suspects

Nine-year-old Kelly and her six-year-old brother David were enduring their parents' difficult divorce and custody battle. When their father picked them up for a weekend visit, they watched their mother wave goodbye, not realizing how long it would be until they saw her again.

Accompanied by their father's girlfriend and the woman's little boy, the group drove for so long that Kelly finally realized something was wrong. She began asking questions. Her father was quiet at first, but then he yelled stinging words. He claimed that her mother didn't love or want the children and that she had given them away.

Life on the run meant moving constantly and living on next to nothing. Thankfully, Kelly's father became worried that his mother (Kelly's grandmother) would be jailed for keeping secrets about their whereabouts. After nearly a year of emotional and physical suffering, Kelly and David returned home.[1]

Kelly is an adult now, and she tells her story on the Web site of Take Root (http://www.takeroot.org/), an organization that teaches about family abduction and helps survivors heal. Countless others can relate to her because more than 200,000 family abductions happen per year.[2] Most don't last more than a month or involve leaving the state to hide.[3] But Kelly's story reflects the problem well because, according to the following data from NISMART-2:

Daniel Porter, right, walks out of a courtroom with his defense attorney. Porter was found guilty of kidnapping after he refused to reveal the whereabouts of his children for two years. He was later charged for their murders. *David Eulitt/AP*

- Young children were most likely to be abducted by family members. For example, 44 percent were under six years old, and 35 percent were between six and 11.
- Forty-two percent of kids abducted by family members were living with a single parent.
- Sixty-three percent of victims were taken while with the abductor, such as during a legal visitation.
- In 53 percent of cases, the biological father abducted the child. Twenty-five percent of abductors were biological mothers.
- Eighty-two percent of family abductors intended to affect custody permanently.
- Abductors rarely used force or threatened to hurt the child. (But this doesn't mean children were not emotionally and physically affected.)
- Almost all children abducted by family members were found, and 91 percent returned home.[4]

THE TRUTH ABOUT FAMILY ABDUCTION

NCMEC defines family abduction as "the taking, keeping, or concealing of a child or children by a parent, other family member, or person acting on behalf of the parent or family member that deprives another individual of his or her custody or visitation rights. Family abductions can occur before or after a court issues a custody determination."[5] Sometimes family abduction is called parental kidnapping, custodial interference, or child snatching.

It is hard to grasp the idea that relatives, the ones who should care most for children, are the most frequent abductors. After all, the kidnappings that make news are often committed by strangers. People who hear about family abductions may think that kids are fine with a parent, or that such cases are private problems that the family should solve. But family abduction is a serious crime with painful results.

In addition to telling the children hurtful lies, some abductors move to unfamiliar surroundings, change kids' names, and mistreat them in other ways. As Take Root executive director Liss Hart-Haviv explains, "You lose everything you've ever loved and known...Your life is gone and your memories become taboo. You become someone else overnight."[6] The more that is learned about

A SURVIVOR'S POEM

I've Come Back To You

I love you Dad

How scary it was that my memory had faded,
Or perhaps I left it behind.
I did remember a few happy times,
But the bad had left my mind.
Regardless of what happened,
The space was still alive.
I knew that nothing would replace him,
So I created my own happy life.
I would imagine the feel of his loving embrace,
The meals he'd make I could almost taste.
She told me once that he had done something wrong,
But I just remember only his song.
'Share the world with human kind,
Never waste a minute of your time,
Keep your thoughts clean and true,
And always remember that I love you.'
Years have passed, and now I know him well;
Every meeting makes my heart swell.
Even when times are at their hardest,
I know now that nothing will ever again part us.

- by Take Root member Jen[7]

family abduction, the clearer it is that finding victims quickly can make a big difference.

INVESTIGATING FAMILIES

NISMART-2 suggests that when police are contacted about family abductions, families usually either know where children are and want them returned, or they need help finding them. To resolve cases, investigators should be familiar with possible motives for family abduction, such as

- The abductor hopes to reunite or have contact with the **left-behind parent**.

- The abductor is afraid of losing custody or visitation rights.
- The abductor wants to blame, spite, or punish the left-behind parent.
- The abductor believes that the child is unsafe at home.
- Occasionally the abductor may be mentally ill.[8]

Investigators should follow many basic steps, such as interviewing people, entering information into the FBI's NCIC database, seeing who has custody, and contacting NCMEC. In these cases, however, it's important to understand specific laws that apply to family abduction, including laws that vary from state to state.

INTERNATIONAL ABDUCTION

According to the U.S. State Department, on April 27, 2004, a mother abducted her two young children and took off for the Middle East. Her trip required at least two flights—one to Europe and another to the Middle East. Thanks to quick action in the United States and abroad, her plans were foiled.

Before the first plane landed, officials in Europe and the Middle East were contacted, and they agreed the mother would not be allowed to continue her trip. Instead, she and her children were put on a flight back to the United States.

At home, the father got custody papers in order and received help from the U.S. Department of State, the FBI, the Department of Homeland Security, and others. Amazingly, the children were back with him the next day. [9]

In an **international abduction,** children from the United States are taken to another country or held in a non-U.S. location. In such cases, legal action plays a big role. The Hague Convention on the Civil Aspects of International Child Abduction (held in 1980) is an agreement among many countries to help victims under age 16 return home quickly.

One of the most important things to do when an international abduction occurs is to contact the U.S. Department of State (also known as the State Department). This part of the government is devoted to foreign affairs and is responsible for protecting and assisting U.S. citizens living or traveling abroad, among other things. If an international abduction occurs, it can

- help parents use the Hague Convention on the Civil Aspects of International Child Abduction when possible
- work to find and check on victims in countries that don't participate in the Hague Convention on the Civil Aspects of International Child Abduction
- give left-behind parents information about other countries' laws and resources

FEELINGS ABOUT FAMILY ABDUCTION

What is it like to be a victim of family abduction? Each person's experience is unique. But NCMEC says it is normal for a child to be upset by

- problems that happened even before the abduction. It's likely that parents had serious difficulties leading up to the abduction.
- moves before or after the abduction. It's hard enough for children to change homes when parents separate or divorce—never mind after being abducted.
- lies that are told, such as "Your mom doesn't love you," and lies the child is compelled to tell, such as, "I've always lived with my dad."
- fear of trusting people, including those who might help. The abductor may teach the child not to be honest with police, doctors, teachers, friends, and others.
- guilt about parents' problems, the abduction, and life after the abduction, even though the child is not at fault.[10]

These are a few of the many reactions children can have to family abduction. Understanding these feelings reminds investigators how worthwhile it is to solve family abduction cases and help children recover.

- tell law enforcement in other countries about concerns that a child might be neglected or abused
- support left-behind parents in many other ways, such as contacting foreign officials and giving updates on how cases are going overseas
- notify the custodial parent if the child applies for a U.S. passport[11]

Of course law enforcement and NCMEC should also be contacted.

Whether an abduction is international or domestic, families need to know that kidnapping doesn't solve family problems: it creates new ones,[12] especially for the child.

Infant Abduction:
The Youngest Victims

On March 31, 2004, the Deseret News in Salt Lake City, Utah, reported that a 39-year-old woman was accused of using scrubs and what looked like a hospital ID to trick a mother into believing her newborn boy was scheduled for a medical procedure. The woman said that she and the infant would return to the hospital room within 20 minutes.

As time passed, the mother grew concerned, and apparently hospital staff did too—some of whom didn't even know a baby was missing. Why was someone who looked like a staff member carrying an infant instead of using standard hospital equipment? Why was a newborn spotted so far from where he should be? And why was a woman in scrubs leaving the hospital with a tiny baby?

Alert employees followed the suspect to a nearby store where a hospital security guard observed her cuddling and rocking the baby. Police arrived quickly, and the woman, who had a long criminal history, was arrested. "She said she didn't have a baby and she was [at the hospital] to get a baby," a police detective said. The infant was returned to his mother within an hour of being taken.[1]

Infant abductions—defined as cases in which a baby six months old or younger is taken by someone outside its family—are so rare that some years they may not happen at all. When they do happen, though, investigators shift their perspective because the crimes often

This photo from a security video shows a woman disguised in medical scrubs abducting an infant from a hospital. *AP*

involve unusual motives and offenders, not to mention the youngest of victims.

THE VICTIMS

It is estimated that between zero and 12 infants (boys and girls about equally) are abducted by nonfamily members each year.[2] That number may sound small, but for the families involved, the effects are enormous. The emotional toll on parents can last long after an infant is found. And even though most infants are returned quickly (research suggests 92 percent are recovered and 75 percent are back in less than five days[3]), that doesn't mean the time away is easy. In addition to being separated from parents, some infants are abandoned.

THE LOCATIONS

Think carefully about the hospital setting. Doctors, nurses, medical assistants, volunteers, and family members are just some of the

♀ WHAT KEEPS INFANTS SAFE?

How do hospitals protect infants? Some security measures need to be kept private. But others are common knowledge, including alarm systems linked to wearable tags. It's important for families to know about recommended policies, such as

- Hospital staff practice what to do if an infant abduction occurs.
- Mothers, fathers, and infants wear matching bands.
- Babies' footprints, bloodwork, and photos are taken to help with proper identification.
- Hospital staff are required to wear official, recognizable identification.
- Visitors check in before seeing babies.
- Families are given safety tips, such as how to verify an employee's identification, and they are encouraged to ask questions.
- Birth announcements are not given to newspapers.[4]

people in a hospital at any given time. With so many responsible people around, it's puzzling that infant abductions happen in hospitals more than anywhere else. One explanation is that abductors blend in with all those strangers, sometimes enough to take infants right from new mothers.[5]

The second most likely location for infant abductions is at home, where many abductors interview for babysitting jobs or pretend to be health care workers.[6] These abductions are more likely to be violent. Occasionally infants are taken from other places, such as a mall or bus station.[7]

THE OFFENDERS

In nonfamily kidnappings overall, the abductors are likely to be male, and the victims are often assaulted.[8] But infant abductions are different. Although investigators shouldn't assume kidnappers will fit a certain profile, NCMEC describes the "typical" infant abductor as someone who

- is female and between 12 and 50 years old
- may be overweight
- lies, deceives, and manipulates others a lot
- often claims she has lost a baby or can't have one
- is likely to be married or living with someone. The partner may want a child, or the abductor may want to have one with him.
- may live near the abduction scene
- frequently does research before the abduction, such as visiting hospitals
- probably plans some aspects of the crime, but may look for opportunities instead of targeting one infant
- might pretend to be a health care employee
- may be familiar with medical staff, hospital routines, and parents of victims
- is capable of caring for the abducted infant[9]

THE PLANS

If a family member announced with no warning at all that she had given birth or adopted a baby, relatives might be shocked. Normally some obvious preparation happens before a baby is born. According to NCMEC, many abductors go to great lengths to fool others into thinking an infant's arrival is natural. They may try to look pregnant, lie about medical appointments, and even have baby showers.[10] But the actual abduction may not be well planned.

THE INVESTIGATION

The FBI says that in June 1988, a woman posing as a nurse took a newborn from a hospital room, saying he needed to be weighed. After medical staff realized what happened, an investigation began and the media was alerted. People called in tips that revealed the baby's location. He was found less than two days later and seemed properly cared for, although his hair had been cut, possibly to hide his identity.[11]

In 2006 word of a similar case spread nationwide about a missing newborn taken from a home where an outdoor sign reportedly announced her birth. The mother said she was assaulted by a woman who fled with the baby.

This two-month-old infant is reunited with her mother after being snatched from her family's minivan in a Wal-Mart parking lot. She was found safe more than 100 miles away. *Donna McWilliam/AP*

While the mother was recovering, a highly publicized search began for the one-week-old girl, who was described as having a red birthmark on her forehead. This information proved vital days later, when a woman contacted officials to say her sister-in-law's baby had makeup covering a red spot, authorities said. Investigators followed up, and the missing infant was found.

"You talk about a lead breaking the case," the sheriff said, "and this was it."[12]

A suspect was arrested and charged with kidnapping and assault. The 36-year-old woman appeared to have some characteristics common to infant abductors, such as losing her own child and living near the crime scene.

The media has a critical role to play in infant abductions because news coverage often generates leads that solve cases.[13] Police work

carefully with reporters to gain the public's help. They also follow standard procedures (such as contacting the FBI and NCMEC,
searching thoroughly, analyzing the crime scene, and conducting
interviews). Hospital security camera footage may reveal clues as
well. Thankfully, the chances of recovering infants are excellent.

Supportive Organizations:
Experts on Call

According to the anti-crime TV show **America's Most Wanted**, *John and Revé Walsh's six-year-old son Adam loved* Star Wars, *baseball, and his beige, oversized captain's hat. He was wearing it on July 27, 1981, when he and his mother headed for the mall to shop for lamps. Adam asked if he could play video games while Revé shopped nearby. She said yes.*

At the video game display, some kids began arguing over the controls. Security arrived and, believing the children's parents were not in the store, sent all the kids outside. It was only minutes later that Revé realized Adam was missing.

The hopeful search for Adam ended two weeks later when part of his remains was found. A medical expert said Adam had probably been killed the day he disappeared. An admitted murderer named Ottis Toole confessed to the crime and recanted (took back his confession) repeatedly, but he was not **prosecuted** *because of lack of physical evidence, some of which had been inexplicably mishandled. Toole later died in prison.*[1]

Exactly what happened to Adam is still a mystery, but its effects on the nation are clear. John and Revé Walsh co-founded the National Center for Missing & Exploited

Adam Walsh's father, John, hosts TV's *America's Most Wanted* and continues to support programs and laws designed to help children in danger. *Joe Marquette/AP*

Children. John hosts America's Most Wanted. *The couple continues to support laws and programs to help endangered children. A country that once lacked a comprehensive response to missing children cases is forever changed.*

Legendary children's TV host Mr. Rogers shared great advice about scary events in the news. "Look for the helpers. You will always find people who are helping." That's what his mother told him when he was little.[2] Thanks to the Walshes and other caring people, helpers abound when a child is abducted. Many families of abducted children have started organizations that fill important needs.

NCMEC

President Ronald Reagan opened the National Center for Missing & Exploited Children (NCMEC), a national child protection resource for families and professionals, in 1984. The Missing Children's Assistance Act (1984) required such a center, and John and Revé Walsh worked hard for its creation. Since then, NCMEC's recovery rate for missing children has reached higher than 96 percent.[3] It has built its success around programs such as

- *Team Adam.* A group of experienced investigators responds to certain critical cases in which children are in danger. Members are retired investigators who go through a special selection process.
- *Project ALERT.* Help from this highly-qualified team (**A**merican's **L**aw **E**nforcement **R**etiree **T**eam) can be requested for many reasons. For example, law enforcement might want assistance with witness interviews or public speaking.
- *The Call Center.* NCMEC staff is always available at 1-800-THE-LOST (1-800-843-5678). Callers who speak another language needn't worry; NCMEC is equipped to handle more than 140 languages.
- *LOCATER.* The **Lo**st **C**hild **A**lert **Te**chnology **R**esource helps law enforcement circulate images and information. One in seven times, NCMEC says, its photo distribution leads to the recovery of a child.
- *The Cold Case Unit.* Long-term cases can be reviewed by specialists, including an expert in **forensic imaging**. An early photo

of a child, for instance, could be changed to show how the child might look today.

- *AMBER Alert.* Time is the enemy in child abduction cases, so NCMEC supports the AMBER Alert system, which informs the public in particularly serious abduction cases.
- *Team HOPE.* This stands for **H**elp **O**ffering **P**arents **E**mpowerment. The group is made up of families who know what it's like to have a missing child. They want to help other families in need.
- *Education.* Because NCMEC wants not only to protect missing and exploited children, but also to protect all children, it raises awareness about child-safety issues.
- *JRLETC.* The **J**immy **R**yce **L**aw **E**nforcement **T**raining **C**enter is named after a Florida boy who was abducted and murdered in 1995. It offers training and technical assistance for professionals who handle missing and exploited children cases.
- *Recovery.* Even after a child is found and the family is reunited, NCMEC is there to help with needs such as transportation, lodging, and follow-up care.[4,5]

In memory of Adam Walsh, NCMEC also supports Code Adam. This program was created by Wal-Mart in 1994 and has become one of the nation's most popular child-safety initiatives. Code Adam can be used when a child disappears in an establishment. Participating locations, such as stores and government agencies, are trained to

- take a detailed description of the missing child and his or her clothing
- use a paging system to announce the Code Adam and share specifics about the child
- watch entrances and look for the child
- alert law enforcement if the child isn't found quickly
- return a child who is lost and unhurt to the family
- prevent anyone found with the child from leaving if possible and safe to do so
- notify law enforcement with a description of a possible abductor seen with the child
- cancel the Code Adam when the situation is resolved or law enforcement arrives[6]

IN THEIR OWN WORDS

"Back in 1981 when Adam was abducted, there weren't any resources for endangered children and their families. My wife Revé and I had no idea what to do. In an instant, our lives were turned completely upside down."[7]

-John Walsh, Adam Walsh's father,
America's Most Wanted and NCMEC

"Walk outside and just take a look around. If everybody did that, think of the miles that you could cover in just five minutes." [8]

-Bob Smither, Laura Smither's father,
Laura Recovery Center[4]

"Not a day goes by when I don't remember how the community came together with unprecedented compassion and support."[9]

-Eve Nichol, Polly Klaas' mother,
the Polly Klaas Foundation

"We can give meaning to Polly's death and create a legacy in her name that will be protective of children for generations to come by pursuing the singular mission of stopping crimes against children."[10]

-Marc Klaas, Polly Klaas' father,
the KlaasKids Foundation and BeyondMissing

"Nothing will ever take away the pain of losing our children...But working to save other missing children helps us give purpose to what would otherwise be senseless and cruel tragedies."[11]

-Erin Runnion, Samantha Runnion's mother,
The Joyful Child Foundation

"I have four main goals:
  1. Fight to change legislation.
  2. Provide a grassroots awareness and continuous support base.

(continues)

(continued)

  3. Search, locate and help law enforcement apprehend absconder pedophiles.
  4. To be with Jessie again."[12]

                    -Mark Lunsford, Jessica Lunsford's father,
                    The Jessica Marie Lunsford Foundation

Over 50,000 locations have joined the Code Adam program, and more can enroll through NCMEC.

THE LAURA RECOVERY CENTER

Early on April 3, 1997, 12-year-old Laura Smither went for a jog alone in her Friendswood, Texas, neighborhood. When she didn't return, thousands of volunteers participated in an unforgettable, nationwide search. Her remains were found 17 days later about 20 miles away. The Laura Recovery Center (LRC) still looks for missing children and provides other services in honor of its first search.

If a student lost something, and the entire school agreed to help look for it, how would the search be organized? Where would volunteers start? Where should they go next? Who should go one way, and who should go another? What if they find something? To whom should they report? Does anyone need special equipment? What if people get hungry or thirsty? Who will handle donations of supplies and money? The fact is that searchers—especially in life or death situations—need organization and guidance. LRC provides this.

The center, co-founded by Laura's parents, "exists to prevent abductions and runaways and to recover missing children by fostering a Triangle of Trust among law enforcement, community and a missing child's family."[13] Each of these groups forms one side of the triangle. Together, they support a common goal: finding the missing child.

Gay Smither, right, co-founder of the Laura Recovery Center, talks with a woman whose daughter and granddaughter were abducted.
Ed Andrieski/AP

Searches depend on many factors, such as case details, location, weather, and volunteers. In some situations, searchers might stand a certain width apart and move forward in a straight line over terrain, while in others, searchers might visit individual homes in a neighborhood.[14] A variety of resources may be needed, such as tracking dogs, helicopters, airplanes, and boats—not to mention basics, such as food and water.

LRC also educates the community and law enforcement about child abduction. In an ideal world, prevention efforts would mean that no more searches were necessary.

OTHER FAMILY-SUPPORTED AGENCIES

Each of the following organizations was founded after the abduction of a child. None of the victims survived, but in every case, a suspect has been charged or convicted.

■ *The Polly Klaas Foundation.* Twelve-year-old Polly Klaas was kidnapped at knifepoint from a slumber party in 1993. Her mother serves on the board of the foundation, which works to protect children and find missing kids.

♀ POWERFUL PICTURES

Many organizations distribute photos to build awareness about abduction cases. Pictures appear on flyers, posters, billboards, television shows, newspaper ads, mailings, and other materials. They are excellent tools for recovering children. These days photos and videos can be shared electronically, which saves valuable time.

NCMEC says the disappearances of Etan Patz (whose father was a photographer), Adam Walsh, and 29 Georgia children in the late 1970s and early 1980s led to photos of children on milk cartons—and eventually a national effort to find missing kids.[15] Law enforcement reports that pictures are "the single most important tool in the search for missing children."[16]

Traditional school portraits are a good example of photos often used in investigations because they're clear, recent, close-ups of the face. Even if a family doesn't order copies of a school picture, one may be available. Some schools partner with Lifetouch studios to make images available to NCMEC when a child is missing and the family requests help.[17]

If a child remains missing and photos become outdated, forensic imaging professionals and technology can help. A photo can be age-enhanced to show what a child might look like over time. The results are impressive.

In one case, a four-year-old girl disappeared with her mother during a custody battle. Thirteen years later, NCMEC professionals age-enhanced her photo, and law enforcement used it to help recognize her.[18] The mother was charged with kidnapping by parent.[19]

In another situation, an age-enhanced photo of an infant victim of family abduction was compared to a driver's license photo and used to help reunite a mother and son after 20 years.[20]

In addition to up-to-date photos, some groups advise parents to collect fingerprints, details about kids (on ID cards), and DNA

■ *The KlaasKids Foundation and BeyondMissing.* Polly's father is the president of KlaasKids, an organization that aims to stop crimes against children, and BeyondMissing, which helps to create and distribute missing child flyers.

(such as by brushing the inside of the cheek with a cotton swab and storing it properly) in case of emergency.

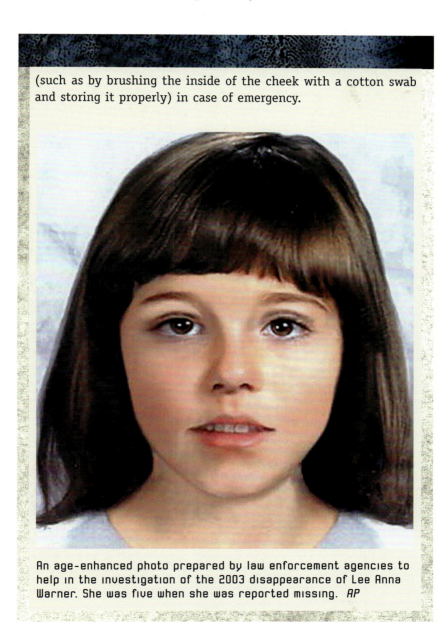

An age-enhanced photo prepared by law enforcement agencies to help in the investigation of the 2003 disappearance of Lee Anna Warner. She was five when she was reported missing. *AP*

- *The Joyful Child Foundation.* After five-year-old Samantha Runnion was abducted while playing outside with a friend, her mother created this foundation to encourage safe and joyful childhoods.
- *The Jessica Marie Lunsford Foundation.* Jessica was kidnapped in the middle of the night. Her father leads an effort to help children in crisis through legislation and other means.
- *The Carole Sund/Carrington Memorial Reward Foundation.* Carole Sund, her daughter, Juli, and another child, Silvina Pelosso, were on a trip to Yosemite National Park when they disappeared. Carole's parents posted reward money in the case, and the group continues to post rewards in missing person investigations.

These are just some of the wide-ranging services NCMEC, LRC, and other agencies provide. They stand as a powerful testament to individuals' strength and determination, even in the face of tragedy.

Recovery:
Healing and Hope

On the evening of June 4, 2002, 14-year-old Elizabeth Smart of Salt Lake City, Utah, attended a year-end awards ceremony at her junior high school. She also received good news from her parents, Ed and Lois. They would let her vacation with a friend's family, something she'd been hoping to do.[1] She even went to bed wearing her favorite red pajamas.

In the middle of the night, however, Elizabeth's life took an unimaginable turn. Her little sister woke her parents with shocking news. An armed man had kidnapped Elizabeth from the girls' bedroom, threatening to kill her sister if she wasn't quiet.

The alarmed Smarts searched the house. Police arrived and considered the possibility that Elizabeth was a runaway. But that wasn't the case. A window screen in the kitchen had been cut, a sibling was a witness, and Elizabeth was a stable girl. Eventually, a Rachael Alert (similar to an AMBER Alert) was issued, and word spread quickly about the case. It was the first time the alert had been used.

In a huge show of support, Laura Recovery Center volunteers and many others searched for Elizabeth with helicopters, dogs, and a poster campaign—not to mention on foot. A reward was offered, the FBI came to help, and images of Elizabeth were shown nationwide. Before long it seemed everyone was looking for Elizabeth and hoping for her safe return.

*Yet days, weeks, and months passed without finding her. Then one day in October 2002, Elizabeth's sister made an incredible announcement. She thought "Immanuel"—a man who had worked briefly on the Smart home—might be the kidnapper. "I was thinking, like, who has been to the house? And who was, like, suspicious?" she said later in an ABC News/*Primetime *television interview. "And the name 'Immanuel' came into my head."[2]*

Immanuel's real name was Brian David Mitchell, and he was married to a woman named Wanda Barzee. Photos of Mitchell were publicized, and on March 12, 2003, witnesses reported seeing him with two people on a Sandy, Utah, street. One was Barzee, and the other was Elizabeth. She was found!

It turned out that on the night Elizabeth was abducted, she had been forced to walk to a distant campsite where she was held captive. Over the next nine months, she was relocated and disguised to hide her identity. She was terribly mistreated. But she survived. It was a real-life, against-the-odds miracle.

Ed and Lois Smart wrote a book about their experiences titled Bringing Elizabeth Home: A Journey of Faith and Hope. *In it they acknowledge that finding Elizabeth isn't the end of the story.[3] When a child is found, there is healing to be done and hope to be offered.*

Investigators work tirelessly to reunite families and abducted children. The FBI clearly states that its top priority in kidnapping cases isn't to catch the kidnappers, but to bring children home safely.[4] But even when a missing child is found, investigators' jobs aren't over, and family life can't just return to normal. In one way, the time after an abduction is similar to the time during an abduction, because cooperation among helpers is essential. Children, families, and investigators shouldn't be expected to recover from such a traumatic experience alone.

BEFORE RECOVERY

The word *recover* has more than one meaning as it relates to child abduction. A child is "recovered" when he or she is officially found

Police composite sketch of a man who called himself "Immanuel" and had worked in the Smart home for one day in November 2001. The sketch was used to track down Brian David Mitchell, Elizabeth's accused kidnapper. *AP*

and protected, in most cases alive. Everyone harmed by abduction must also "recover" from it. Neither task is easy, and both require preparation.

A helpful step is to create a team that specializes in recovery and **reunification** (bringing families back together). According to NCMEC, such a team should

- *Have members with a variety of skills.* It might include trained representatives of law enforcement, courts, child protective/ social services, mental health agencies, the school system, and victim-witness offices, which help victims through court procedures and may arrange compensation for certain costs.
- *Understand the effects of abduction.* Each case is different, depending on how long it lasted, what occurred, and how the child and family cope. Circumstances around the abduction can have an impact too. For example, did parents separate before a family abduction?

President Bush greets Elizabeth Smart, center, and her mother, Lois, in the Roosevelt Room at the White House in April 2003. *Eric Draper/AP*

- *Plan carefully, but be flexible.* It may not be necessary for every team member to help right away. After a child is found, various skills will be required, based on the details of the case. Experts should figure out what kinds of help are needed and provide them as soon as possible.[5]

These are just a few of the NCMEC-recommended characteristics of a strong recovery and reunification team. The organization is there to help law enforcement agencies and other officials prepare for the many potential challenges of reunification.

DURING RECOVERY

One thing is more important than any other when a child is recovered: caring for the victim. Yet research shows that in 80 percent of missing child recoveries, victims get no psychological support.[6] On the positive side, there are many ways to treat the child carefully, keeping in mind that abduction can involve a variety of stresses. For example, NCMEC suggests that officials

- *Be ready to comfort and reassure the child.* When Elizabeth Smart was found, police reassured her not to be afraid.[7] Fear of officials—and even loved ones—is understandable because kidnappers may have encouraged victims to feel this way.
- *Meet the child's physical and psychological needs.* The child may have immediate, basic needs (such as a clean outfit), and he or she may need a medical evaluation. (Elizabeth Smart's mother was with her for this, and the hospital provided a change of clothes.[8]) A mental health specialist can also help prepare the child for reunification.
- *Interview the child.* This is one of the first things that happened in the Smart case.[9] It's important for officials to understand what the child experienced and what crimes were committed. An expert should be part of this process, since interviewing children involves special skills, and poor questioning can hurt children emotionally.
- *Protect privacy.* Many people need to be notified when a child is recovered, including the family and perhaps the media. But reunification should happen in a private, calm setting. The Smarts were given a room at the police station for this purpose.[10]

⚲ MORE REASONS TO HOPE

Case One: According to *TIME* magazine, something unusual happened at a birthday party on January 24, 2004. A woman attending the party noticed that a little girl bore a strong resemblance to the woman's newborn, who had supposedly died in a house fire six years earlier. She had always suspected that her baby was abducted right before the fire started, but others thought that was wishful thinking.

Now she was so certain of the girl's identity that she took a sample of the child's hair by pretending to pull gum from it. Investigators were willing to see if their DNA matched. It did. The woman found her kidnapped child without an investigation ever taking place.[11] The family was reunited with the help of experts, and a distant relative was charged in the case.[12] She was sentenced to nine to 30 years in prison.[13]

Case Two: On March 2, 1998, in Austria, a 10-year-old girl disappeared on her way to school. Her fate remained a mystery for eight years, until August 2006. That's when the young woman escaped her alleged kidnapper and revealed that she had been kept in a cellar much of the time. How did she free herself? Her 44-year-old captor reportedly became distracted by a phone call and a noisy vacuum cleaner, and that (combined with an unlocked door) provided an opportunity to run to a neighbor's home.[14] The man later committed suicide. The young woman's recovery was expected to be difficult,[15] but her extraordinary homecoming was something to celebrate.

It's helpful to bring memorable items from home, such as family photos or a favorite stuffed animal. The media should not be present.

■ *Keep everyone informed.* Unfamiliar situations can be intimidating, but they're not quite as difficult if someone explains them first. Children and families should be told what to expect. For instance, parents might be informed that their child's appearance has changed since the abduction, as Elizabeth Smart's had.[16]

- *Be aware of special issues.* In family abduction cases, different concerns may arise, such as the child being afraid because of an abductor's lies about the left-behind parent, the child not remembering the left-behind family, or the child feeling protective of the abductor. Sometimes a child does not even remember his or her original name. From the child's point of view, reunification can be so upsetting that it feels like another abduction. Steps must be taken to help the child cope.[17]

AFTER RECOVERY

Once a child has been recovered, police can cancel some requests they have made for help with the case, such as AMBER Alerts or NCIC entries. But if an abductor hasn't been caught, police may work for years or even decades to solve the crime.

The Amber Hagerman case, which inspired the AMBER Alert, is an example of long-term police commitment. In 2006, 10 years after Amber's life was taken, lead investigating officer Sgt. Mark Simpson told the *Dallas Morning News*, "Whoever did this is still out there somewhere," and "The only date I'll attach any significance to is the arrest date."[18]

When an alleged abductor is caught, good investigation can contribute to a successful prosecution in court. During this process, experts should help the child and family—not only with the emotional effects of abduction, but also with navigating the court system. If the child has to testify in court, special accommodations may be made, such as touring the courtroom ahead of time or testifying by closed-circuit television rather than in the courtroom itself.

When a defendant—the person accused of committing a crime—is found guilty in a case related to kidnapping, he or she is given some type of sentence. This varies from situation to situation. If a murder has been committed, the sentence is often death, as it was in the infamous Lindbergh baby, Megan Kanka, and Polly Klaas abductions. Prison terms may last a lifetime. In the Smart case, Brian Mitchell and Wanda Barzee were ruled unfit to stand trial, but this could change after they receive mental health treatment while hospitalized.[19] Family abductions, meanwhile, have a wide range of results that depend on many factors.

No matter what the outcome of a case, investigators should review how it was handled. What worked? What needs to be improved? Law enforcement personnel also deserve psychological support to deal with the stress of abduction cases. Recovering well from each case offers hope for future success.

Prevention:
Use What You Know

USA TODAY *reported that 14-year-old Stephanie Quackenbush was only a block away from school when a man grabbed her, covered her face with a towel, and threatened to stab her if she wasn't quiet. That didn't stop her from yelling and fighting back. People nearby heard what was going on and came to the rescue. The man took off, but he left a key piece of evidence—the towel. His DNA was on it. The man was identified as Darius Ashley, and Quackenbush testified at his trial. He was also linked to two other abductions. Now he is sentenced to 25 years in prison.*

Quackenbush now speaks out to help other kids.[1] Her advice is to "fight back, scream as hard as you can. You have one chance, why not take it."[2]

Another abduction attempt occurred while 12-year-old Mickenzie Smith and her younger brother were riding bikes. A man pulled up in his truck and began talking to them. He said he had lost his dog. Mickenzie sensed something was wrong and guided her brother away, but the man pulled her into his truck. Mickenzie followed advice she had heard, plus her own **instincts***, and turned on her attacker, screaming and attacking him as he drove. While this was happening, her brother ran to a nearby house to call 911. Soon the man—later identified as Damon Crist—pulled over and let Mickenzie out. He was later caught and sentenced to at least 10 years in prison.*

There are few times in life when it's okay to be loud and disruptive, but escaping abduction is one of them. Stephanie and Mickenzie recognized this and lived to describe their experiences. NCMEC presented them with National Courage Awards in 2006.

The girls demonstrated something that NCMEC analysis reflects. In 403 cases in which children escaped attempted abductions

- Sixty percent of kids reacted by yelling, kicking, pulling away, or getting other people's attention.
- Thirty percent of children got away by walking or running from the scene without physical contact with the suspect.
- Ten percent of kids received help from another person who intervened.[3]

In addition, NCMEC found that attempted nonfamily abductions by strangers happen more often

- when a child is traveling to or from school or a school-related activity
- to girls than boys
- to children between 10 and 14 years old
- with suspects using a vehicle[4]

COMMON PLOYS

Stephanie and Mickenzie also experienced another aspect of abduction: Kidnappers frequently try to fool children into cooperating with them. In Stephanie's case, the offender tried unsuccessfully to scare her into silence. In Mickenzie's case, the man said his dog was lost. She didn't fall for it. Many safety advocates advise kids to recognize tricks such as

- *Asking for help.* "My arm is broken. Can you help me carry this box?" "Will you help me look for my lost pet?" "How do I get to the grocery store from here?" Kids can escape risky situations without even answering such questions. The adult should find someone older to help if needed, and the child should report the problem to a parent or other safe adult.
- *Making offers.* Lots of things tempt children—money, rides, candy, alcohol, drugs, cigarettes, pets, jobs, fun activities. No mat-

ter how appealing an offer or person seems, choose safety instead. Get away and consult a parent, guardian, or trusted adult.

- *Giving orders.* "Your mom is in the hospital. Quick, come with me!" "Your dad sent me to pick you up." "I'm a police officer. Get in the car." "Hey Joe, come here." Make sure unexpected developments are real, and plan with family members about how emergencies will be handled. When authorities are involved, look for official uniforms and marked cars. Also realize that offenders may see names on personal items, so put identifying information in hidden spots only.

SAFETY CHOICES

Recognizing danger is important—and so is reacting to it. Keep in mind that warning signs can be subtler than threats or lures. The simple feeling that something "isn't right" deserves immediate attention. The challenge is to be safe, even if it's embarrassing or difficult. It's worth it! Popular suggestions include

- *Trust instincts.* There is no single definition of a dangerous situation. If a situation *feels* unsafe, scary, or uncomfortable, trust that feeling.
- *Get away.* Escape inappropriate requests, offers, instructions, and overtures. Find a safe place fast and tell a trusted adult.
- *Be willing to be rude.* It's fine to be more than impolite in the name of safety. Children can say *No!*, disobey, scream, kick, run away, attract attention, and more.
- *Yell and tell.* These two little words represent a lot of power. They are important ways to get attention and help.
- *Head for safety.* If being followed by a car, go in the opposite direction toward a safer situation. Report what happened.
- *Plan ahead with adults.* If children walk to school, for example, families should choose the safest route available. Identify places to go in case assistance is needed.
- *Stay in public.* Refuse to be taken away. Abductors change locations to get control over victims and commit further crimes.
- *Seek help.* Kids can yell something like, "This is not my father!" or "This is not my mother!" This may encourage others to get involved.

- *Keep in touch.* Parents and caregivers must always be aware of children's plans and whereabouts. Family members should know how to find and reach each other.
- *Stick with others.* Being in a pair or group isn't a guarantee of safety, but it's a step in the right direction.
- *Practice, practice, practice.* A good way to build safety skills is to practice them, such as through imagining ("What if…?"), discussing, and role-playing (acting).
- *Be empowered.* Abduction is very unlikely. Put your mind at ease with knowledge and abilities. Live in confidence, not fear.

♀ PREVENTING FAMILY ABDUCTION

What about family abductions in which a parent is the abductor? How can they be prevented? According to the U.S. Department of Justice, some possible recommendations include

- obtain specific court orders about custody, visitation, travel, and consequences for violations
- keep legal paperwork immediately available
- make sure relatives understand laws related to helping a parent abduct
- protect passports, such as by having an unbiased party keep them for the family
- share court orders with providers of passports and birth certificates
- check accusations of child abuse carefully to protect children and be fair to parents
- offer counseling that helps families through difficult times[5]

Decisions about how to keep kids safe depend on families' unique situations. The most serious steps are saved for times when a child is at particular risk for abduction, harm, or being taken to a remote or difficult-to-access location, such as another country.[6] Meanwhile, there are many more ways judges, social workers, school staff, and others work to prevent family abduction. NCMEC also recommends that children know how much they are loved, and how to reach trusted adults if necessary.[7]

ARE ALL "STRANGERS" DANGEROUS?

Many children are given a well-meaning but outdated warning: "Don't talk to strangers!" Believe it or not, this warning can be dangerous itself because

- *It isn't sensible.* Children and adults have to deal with strangers frequently—when they meet a new classmate, when they ask a librarian a question, when they make purchases, and countless other times. It's not practical to avoid all strangers.
- *The word "stranger" can be confusing.* When kids hear it, they may imagine someone who looks obviously scary. In reality, strangers with bad intentions can look pretty ordinary.
- *Strangers can be helpful.* Imagine a lost or abducted child who needs help. Talking to a stranger could be the key to safety. A woman or a mother with children, for example, might be a good choice. There are plenty of fine strangers.
- *Strangers aren't the only problem.* While strangers certainly can be dangerous, children often know the people who commit crimes against them.

Instead of relying on an old rule criticized by experts, use instincts, good judgment, and safety skills—and turn to parents, guardians, and other trusted adults for help.

TESTING, TESTING

Some experts "test" children's safety skills to educate the public about crime and how kids should be protected. A memorable 1993 episode of *The Oprah Winfrey Show* showed Ken Wooden, a leading child-safety advocate, enticing young children away from a park to find a puppy (although they weren't in real danger) while shocked parents, who had agreed to an experiment, watched from a distance.[8]

Many other "tests" have been done since, and the results are just as striking. In 2006 Wooden and CBS' *The Early Show* used various lures with much older kids—college students. Wooden offered them modeling screen tests in a van (some got in), asked kids to look at police evidence in a van (some got in), requested help loading boxes into a van (some helped), and told kids he would pay

Midsi Sanchez, 8, and her mother, Susana Velasco, lead a group
of family and friends back to their Vallejo, California, home after
attending Mass on a Sunday in August 2000. Midsi was a kidnap
victim just three days before, but managed to escape by finding keys
to her handcuffs in her captive's car and flagging down a truck on a
nearby road. *Mike Jory/AP*

them to ride in a van and give him directions (some got in). Many students had something in common other than falling for Wooden's lures. They felt fear or uneasiness. The message: Learn about lures and trust instincts.[9]

Another test was conducted by safety expert and former police officer Bob Stuber. With parent permission and supervision, he knocked on kids' doors, said his cat was in the backyard, and asked if he could come in to get it. Every child let him in the house. He wants home-alone children to know, "Keep the door shut and locked at all times."[10] He also advises children being abducted to be creative. In a car, for instance, if the child can't get out a front door, back doors are an option too.[11]

In a separate experiment recorded by ABC News, Stuber challenged teenage girls at a mall. He told them he was part of a reality show, and that the girls' parents said he could follow them and see where they shopped. But when he claimed a parent was in his van and asked the girls to come with him, they said no—even when he tried to talk them into it.[12]

Home alarm systems require installation and money. But humans come with a free, built-in alarm system that warns about danger. When this system sends a signal—such as fear or an uncomfortable feeling—react boldly instead of freezing. Do what it takes to stay safe. Knowledge and power are a potent combination.

The Internet:
Protection through Privacy

When the FBI describes the history of its Innocent Images National Initiative (**IINI**), which protects children from sexual *predators* online, it begins with the story of a missing child.

In 1993 investigators were searching for a 10-year-old boy who disappeared in Brentwood, Maryland. While conducting door-to-door interviews in his neighborhood, they met two men who had paid significant attention to area kids—giving them gifts and even vacationing with them. Evidence suggested the men had been abusing children for decades, and they'd found a new way to target children: going online.[1]

Today's version of the Internet didn't exist, but the men still found ways to exchange sexual pictures, communicate with children, and arrange in-person meetings.[2] Further investigation led to more and more *pedophiles* online. Before long, the FBI realized there were online predators across the nation.

IINI was launched in 1995 and dedicated to the missing boy, who hasn't been found, "and to the countless victims of child sexual exploitation over the years."[3]

THE IINI TODAY

The IINI has come a long way since its start. The FBI reports that in fiscal year 1996, 113 cases were opened. Compare that to 2,135 in fiscal year 2006—a 1,789 percent increase. In that time a total of 17,691 cases were opened.[4]

An investigation often begins after a problem is reported by a citizen, online service provider, or law enforcement agency—or when simply the name of an online location raises concern.[5] Using a variety of methods and international resources, IINI works to

- find and hold responsible people who sexually exploit children online
- stay on the Internet to prevent sexual exploitation of children
- protect children who have already been victimized[6]

To catch online predators, investigators may go undercover—sometimes posing as kids—and collect evidence from chats or

☿ WHAT IF SOMETHING UNCOMFORTABLE HAPPENS ONLINE?

Unfortunately, preventative steps such as learning about Internet safety and using protective software do not guarantee a perfect online experience. Sometimes kids are surprised by what appears, uninvited, on the computer screen. When this happens, what should they do?

First, trust instincts. If something feels wrong, report it to parents, Internet service providers, and authorities. Keep evidence available for investigators. (For example, don't delete an upsetting email. Turn off the monitor if something disturbing appears.[7]) Certain incidents should always be reported to local law enforcement, the FBI, and NCMEC, such as receiving

- sexual pictures of children
- sexual solicitations knowingly sent to a child under 18
- sexual images knowingly sent to a child under 18[8]

The FBI can be reached at http://www.fbi.gov and 202-324-3000. NCMEC can be reached at http://www.cybertipline.com and 1-800-THE-LOST (1-800-843-5678). CyberTipline reports are shared with the FBI and other helpful agencies. Making a CyberTipline report is easy, and it can make a difference for kids everywhere.

emails. In one chat, for example, an agent pretended to be a 13-year-old girl staying home from school sick. A man chatted with her for more than an hour, sent her a photo, and asked if she had a computer in her bedroom. His behavior stood out enough to get the FBI's attention.[9]

Although going online is a fun and helpful activity, it can also be risky. But it's good to know the FBI is serious about online safety, and so are many other law enforcement agencies, which often receive training from the FBI.

INTERNET CRIMES AGAINST CHILDREN TASK FORCE PROGRAM

There are at least 46 teams across the country cooperating with the FBI and NCMEC to target online dangers. These Internet Crimes Against Children (**ICAC**) Task Forces are funded by the U.S. Department of Justice's Office of Juvenile Justice and Delinquency Programs, and they have made significant progress, with more than 1,600 arrests in 2005.[10] They not only investigate cases, but also educate communities and help victims.

In one success story described by NCMEC, someone met a man online who wanted help seeing a 14-year-old girl in Minnesota. The girl also requested help arranging the meeting. Instead, the person in touch with both people contacted NCMEC's **CyberTipline**, which takes reports about child sexual exploitation. NCMEC, the Minnesota ICAC Task Force, and Minneapolis-St. Paul International Airport Police worked quickly to identify and stop the man, who flew into town with a new phone for the girl (so they could talk secretly) and possible criminal intentions.[11]

PRETEENS, TEENS, AND THE INTERNET

It's no surprise that NCMEC is among groups leading the charge to understand and prevent the dangers kids face online. In 2006, it published *Online Victimization of Youth: Five Years Later*, a follow-up to *Online Victimization: A Report on the Nation's Youth*. These reports are based on **Youth Internet Safety Surveys** (*YISS-1* and *YISS-2*) done in 1999-2000 and 2005. In *YISS-2* researchers talked with kids between 10 and 17 years old after getting permission from parents or guardians. The survey showed that

- Eighty-six percent of youth had used the Internet in the past week.
- Kids spent online time visiting Web sites (99 percent), doing schoolwork (92 percent), playing games (83 percent), emailing (79 percent), instant messaging (68 percent), downloading music (38 percent), going to chat rooms (30 percent), journaling or blogging (16 percent), and using dating or romance sites (1 percent).
- Online, 79 percent of youth talked to people they knew in real life, and 34 percent talked to people they only knew online.

Former New Jersey Attorney General Peter C. Harvey presents an Internet predator safety program. During the program, designed to alert students and their parents to the dangers of predators on the Internet, Harvey showed a message from a middle-aged man who posed as a 14-year-old girl named Jenny. *Mike Derer/AP*

- Thirteen percent of children (about 1 in 7) were sexually approached (talked to or asked about sex when they did not want to discuss it) or solicited (asked to do sexual things they didn't want to do) on the Internet.
- Four percent of youth Internet users received "aggressive" sexual solicitations in which they were telephoned, sent real-life objects (gifts or money), or asked to meet in person. In rare cases, these children were sexually assaulted.
- Four percent of youth Internet users received "distressing" sexual solicitations that seriously upset or scared them.
- Two percent of youth Internet users were solicited in ways that were both "aggressive" and "distressing."
- More girls (70 percent) than boys (30 percent) were approached or solicited sexually.
- Kids 13 and older (90 percent) were more likely to be victims of sexual approaches and solicitations.
- Thirty-nine percent of kids reported that solicitors were adults. Most solicitors overall (73 percent) were male.
- Nine percent of youth Internet users reported being harassed online, which involved being worried, embarrassed, or threatened. One 10-year-old boy said, "This person, she gave me her address and told me to come over. I said no, and then she started typing in bad words. [It happened because] there are a lot of people out there that do a lot of stuff…. I think they were trying to make me come over there to kidnap me."[12]

ABDUCTION AND THE INTERNET

Children are on the Internet a lot—and so are people who put them at risk. But is kidnapping a real concern? According to NCMEC, "The number of teens who are molested, abducted, or leave home as a result of contacts made on the Internet are relatively low, but when it happens the results can be tragic."[13] The following story is proof.

Thirteen-year-old Kacie Woody of Holland, Arkansas, didn't have an easy start in life. As a baby, she survived a life-threatening illness. As a seven year old, she lost her mother in a car accident. But her spirit was unbreakable. She was a cheerful, loving daughter whose family adored her.

Kacie loved to write poetry. One of her poems begins, "I am an angel, sent from above, to spread the world, with lots of love." While she had an active middle-school social life, Kacie also enjoyed meeting people online. One of them was a boy from Georgia with whom she chatted often.

On the night of December 3, 2002, the pair was instant messaging. Kacie was home alone, and she was also on the phone with Dave, a guy she met in a chat room over the summer. She wasn't allowed to talk with him online because of his age, which he said was 18, but he had started calling. Kacie cried with him as he talked about an aunt who was dying.

Kacie's school counselor had warned her that day about Internet dangers.[14] Part of the conversation between Kacie (modelbehavior63) and the Georgia boy (Tazz2999) referred to the counselor's advice:

modelbehavior63: *so guess what i got. . . a lecture*

Tazz2999: *awww im sorry baby*

modelbehavior63: *. . .on how u could be a 80 year old rapest. . . lol*

Tazz2999: *lol*

modelbehavior63: *hehe. . . and that the picture was ur grandson*

Tazz2999: *how many times have u gotten that 1 hehe*

modelbehavior63: *um. . . i lost count. . .well. . . then. . . she is like . . ."do ur parents know u talk to ppl u dont know" i was like "yeah" and she was like. . .well be careful. . . and dont agree to meet them less ur mom or dad is with you" i was like. . . okay. . . and she is like. . . well remember this lil talk. . . i was like. . . ok. . .*

Tazz2999: *uh oh. prolly means she is going to talk to u again . . .*

modelbehavior63: *i kno*

They talked about other things, including their relationship:

Tazz2999: *hehe ill always be with u my angel becouse ur all I want to be with*

Tazz2999: *hehe i put my screen saver as the picture i have in my locker*
Tazz2999: *ur the most beutiful angel in the world Kacie*
Tazz2999: *r u ok sweetie?*

Suddenly Kacie had stopped responding. Her last message was short: "yah." The boy kept instant messaging her, trying to understand her silence. She didn't answer because something was terribly wrong.

Dave, who Kacie believed was a teenage friend, was actually 47-year-old David Fuller of California. He had tracked down Kacie, entered her house, and abducted her. He didn't have an aunt who was dying. He had used that story to get close to Kacie. A photo of him online was really of his nephew.[15]

When Kacie's brother returned home, he realized something was wrong and called their father, an on-duty police officer. Almost immediately, an investigation began. An alert similar to an AMBER Alert was issued.

It didn't take long for investigators to make the connection between Kacie and Dave. The family computer held records of their online communications.

On December 4, after visiting area motels, investigators were confident Dave was in town. He had rented a room, a van, and a local storage unit. When officials arrived at the unit, a gunshot was heard. Dave had committed suicide. He had already sexually assaulted and shot Kacie.

Kacie did not survive her abduction. But her goodness lives on through the Kacie Woody Foundation, which teaches about Internet predators and safety. Its Internet Predator Awareness Team is made up of kids who educate students, parents, teachers, and law enforcement officers with help from Kacie's father, Rick Woody. He has been honored by the FBI for his community leadership.[16]

It turned out that Kacie wasn't Dave's only target. He had pursued other teens online. One refused to give him her phone number.[17] That's just the kind of thing the Kacie Woody Foundation wants other kids to do.[18]

Rick Woody holds a picture of his late daughter at his home near Greenbrier, Arkansas. Woody's daughter Kacie was kidnapped and murdered by David Fuller, a man she met in an Internet chat room. *Mike Wintrooth/AP*

ONLINE PRECAUTIONS

Experts don't want children to avoid the Internet altogether. It's an incredible resource that should be used and appreciated. But just like in the "real world," there are unsafe situations, areas, and people online. And just like in the real world, some of these risks are disguised. Some are tempting, too, especially to people feeling lonely, reckless, trusting, or simply curious. Youth Internet users are encouraged to

■ *Keep personal information private.* This includes all kinds of identifying information, such as name, address, phone number, school, job, photos, and details about family and friends. Remember to pick a non-revealing screen name.

- *Be skeptical.* No matter how believable people are online, they could be lying. Someone who seems like a funny, understanding 15-year-old girl, for example, could be a middle-aged man with disturbing motives.
- *Report concerns.* Tell parents about uncomfortable online experiences. Other good resources include local law enforcement, the FBI, and NCMEC. NCMEC has a special reporting area at cybertipline.com.
- *Resist responding to negative messages.* When a child is sent something inappropriate or odd, it isn't his or her fault. It is best to let responsible adults, such as parents or authorities, take over.
- *Set limits on meetings.* Meeting online-only "friends" in person is not recommended. If a meeting is considered, involve parents or guardians ahead of time, bring them along, and choose a public meeting spot.
- *Double check with parents.* Even if a download, pop-up window, new email address, request for information, or anything else seems legitimate, check with a parent or guardian. Many online tricks are used to jeopardize privacy and security.
- *Socialize with safety in mind.* Communicate online with true offline friends. Use features like privacy settings and passwords to help. But think of online posts as public—and permanent.
- *Beware of chats.* Chatrooms are believed to be especially dangerous. "To put it bluntly," NCMEC says, "chatrooms—especially those used by teenagers—are sometimes also used by child molesters to find victims."[19]
- *Agree on Internet rules.* Families need to talk openly about Internet issues. For example, when are kids allowed to be online? What information is considered private? Team up with friends, too. Commit to protecting each other's privacy and well-being.

The Internet has changed a great deal since its creation. Many new uses—both good and bad—are surely in store. As time passes, online safety needs to improve along with the Internet's features. Kids can join investigators and other experts in promoting online choices that enhance—not endanger—real-life success.

The Adult Victim:
Someone's Child

It was June 1997, and North Carolina State University design student Kristen Modafferi had just turned 18. She was in San Francisco for a summer of working and studying. Just a few weeks following her arrival, however, she disappeared after leaving the coffee shop where she worked. There was a frustrating lack of clues about her disappearance.

Because Kristen was 18, she didn't qualify as a missing child, and her family couldn't access the same resources available to families of younger missing kids. As a result, supporters pushed for Kristen's Act, which passed in 2000 and became **Kristen's Law**. *It helped to establish the National Center for Missing Adults (*NCMA*).*

NCMA collects and shares information about missing adults who seem at risk, helps law enforcement and families find missing adults, and promotes missing adult causes in many other ways. It still publicizes Kristen's unsolved case as part of its work.

The story of 19-year-old Suzanne Lyall has similarities to Kristen's case.

Suzanne was a college sophomore in New York when she disappeared on March 2, 1998. The computer whiz left her job at a software store after 9:00 p.m., took a short bus ride, and then disappeared.

Suzanne's ATM card was used the next afternoon in a local store. Police looked for a man who bought something around the same time, but they were unsuccessful, even though they released a composite picture of him and the Nike cap he was wearing.[1]

Since Suzanne was over 17, she wasn't considered a missing child. That meant police did not have to investigate her disappearance right away.[2] "When someone disappears," her parents wrote on a Web site, "time is of the essence in investigating...We know, as indeed most parents would know, that there was something terribly wrong. We didn't need a waiting period, and the law should not encourage one."[3]

*In 2003 **Suzanne's Law** was passed as part of the PROTECT Act, which strengthens law enforcement's ability to fight crimes against children. Under Suzanne's Law, authorities must enter information about missing persons under the age of 21 into the FBI's NCIC computer database. Suzanne remains missing.*

Every kidnapped or missing person is someone's child. Laws named after Kristen and Suzanne recognize that when kids become adults, their safety should still be a national priority.

Regrettably, NCMA says the cost of its work and lack of funding, particularly after Hurricane Katrina left so many victims behind, put the organization itself at risk. In 2006 it sought public support to continue its services.

Many missing and abducted adults need help. The number of active missing-adult cases changes constantly, but in April 2006, the FBI's NCIC total was more than 50,000.[4] While most missing adults are not kidnapping victims (many suffer from addictions, dementia, or mental illness[5]), some have been abducted. The total number of adults kidnapped each year is not clear.[6]

ABDUCTION MOTIVES

Kidnapped children are most often victims of family abduction, but adults are usually taken for different reasons. According to Michael Newton's *The Encyclopedia of Kidnappings*, some possible motives for abduction include

- *Protection.* Sometimes a criminal committing another offense (such as robbery) takes a hostage, believing this will shield the offender or help with escape.

- *Money.* A victim might be held for ransom or have valuables stolen. Rarely, one family member takes another in order to get profits, such as retirement income.
- *Sexual assault.* Some kidnapped people become victims of sex crimes.
- *Nonsexual assault.* An abductor might intend to hurt or kill the victim. This could be for revenge, terrorism, or other purposes.
- *Slavery.* A captive might be forced to work and earn money for the kidnapper.

♀ THE PATTY HEARST KIDNAPPING

Patty Hearst is one of the most memorable adult kidnapping victims in U.S. history. She is also a survivor.

It was February of 1974 when 19-year-old Patty, the granddaughter of a wealthy newspaper publisher, was kidnapped from her apartment in Berkeley, California. Her abductors were members of the Symbionese Liberation Army (SLA), a violent terrorist group that demanded free food for the needy. Patty's father, Randolph Hearst, agreed to help.

About two months later, there were shocking developments in the case. Patty appeared on video calling herself "Tania," criticizing her family, and saying she had joined the SLA. She also helped the SLA rob a bank at gunpoint. Footage from a surveillance camera was proof.

Controversy raged about Patty's actions. Was she a victim or a criminal? Did she have Stockholm syndrome, a psychological reaction in which victims begin to connect with their captors? Had she been **brainwashed**?

It took more than a year to find Patty, but when the FBI located her in September 1975, she was arrested. Eventually, she was convicted of robbery and sentenced to seven years in prison. Two abductors were convicted in her kidnapping. Other SLA members had since died in violent confrontations.

Patty claimed she had been brutally assaulted and brainwashed. In 1979 President Jimmy Carter commuted her sentence, and she was released. In 2001 President Bill Clinton granted her a pardon.

⚲ STRANGE STORIES

Every once in a while, an adult kidnapping—or a *supposed* kidnapping—makes headlines not just because a startling crime is reported, but because the apparent motives stand out. Two cases involved brides in very different situations.

In 2005 Jennifer Wilbanks, known as the "Runaway Bride," disappeared days before her planned April wedding, saying she had been kidnapped—a tale authorities doubted. She later admitted leaving on her own. According to CNN, Wilbanks' sentence included probation, community service, payments to the sheriff's department, and continued mental health treatment.[7] "Wilbanks stated that she could not be the wife that her fiancé John Mason needed," an FBI report said. "Wilbanks wanted to disappear without a trace."[8] The relationship with her fiancé did not last.

In 2006 a couple was accused of kidnapping their daughter to stop her August wedding. Although Julianna Redd was gone two days and missed her original wedding ceremony, she did marry her fiancé. *USA TODAY* reported that Utah County Attorney Kay Bryson said, "I've never had a case quite like this ... It is strange that parents would go to that extent to keep an adult daughter from marrying the man that she had chosen to marry."[9] The parents were charged with second-degree felony kidnapping and faced the possibility of 15 years in prison.

- *Other demands.* Criminals who hold airline passengers hostage, for example, may insist on flying to a certain location or having friends released from prison.
- *Other purposes.* Interrogation (questioning) is among a variety of additional motives for kidnapping.[10]

THE LAW ENFORCEMENT RESPONSE

Adults vanish for many reasons other than kidnapping, so it is a challenge for law enforcement to figure out which situations are most serious. Limited resources mean every case cannot be a top concern. Investigators also realize that many adults leave home willingly, and some people do not want to be found.

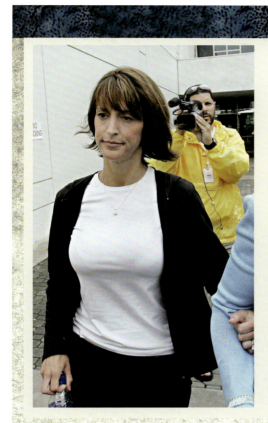

Jennifer Wilbanks, whose disappearance days before her 2005 wedding earned her the "Runaway Bride" moniker, leaves the Gwinnett County courthouse in Lawrenceville, Georgia. Wilbanks originally claimed that she was kidnapped but later admitted to leaving on her own. *Ric Feld/AP*

NCMEC's Team HOPE, a group of volunteers whose children are or have been missing, tells families of missing adults, "Some law enforcement agencies are reluctant to take a report of a missing adult," and "Most often with adult missing, the families do the majority of the searching."[11] These developments can be extremely frustrating to families who are desperate to find loved ones.

In the state of Washington, a series of newspaper articles looked at how missing persons investigations were being handled. *Seattle Post-Intelligencer* reporters found problems with the system, and officials soon took action.[12] A government task force created a "toolbox" of information to help police and citizens in these cases.[13] This is a good example of progress.

Keep in mind that most missing adults are not victims of crime.[14] But if there are signs that an adult is kidnapped or in some type of danger, law enforcement is likely to take certain basic steps. Investigators may

- *Conduct interviews.* Family, friends, and others can provide important specifics about the person and where they were last seen.
- *Collect details.* Some examples include social security number, vehicle, clothing, habits, mood, cell phone number, health, and activities.
- *Search.* Clues can lead investigators to numerous locations. Hospitals should also be checked.
- *Request photos.* These can be used in a variety of ways, including on missing person posters.
- *Enter the case into NCIC.* If authorities find someone, his or her description might match a listing in this FBI database.
- *Preserve evidence.* It is important to keep items that may contain DNA, such as a toothbrush or hairbrush. Dental records and fingerprints help too.
- *Check finances.* Did the missing person leave with or without money? When were credit cards and bank accounts last used?

Abducted children of all ages deserve to have dedicated professionals working on their behalf. Thankfully, law enforcement, families, volunteers, researchers, and others focus not only on finding victims, but also on finding answers to fundamental questions such as

- *Who are abducted children?* Innocent victims from newborns to young adults.
- *Who kidnaps them?* Family members, people they know, and strangers.
- *Why are they taken?* Frequent motives are related to custody and assault.
- *Most importantly, how can this problem be solved?* By using every available resource, from federal programs to individual instincts and creating new solutions.

Child abduction and kidnapping have long been a painful reality. But they are not an end in and of themselves. Whether an investigation leads to joy, despair, or more questions than answers, it can also bring wisdom that protects the lives of others.

Chronology

1874 Charley and Walter Ross, ages four and six, are kidnapped near Germantown, Pennsylvania. Walter is found but Charley is not. News of the abduction, America's first major ransom kidnapping, spreads across the country and raises concerns about this emerging crime. The main suspects die without being tried.

1932 Charles Augustus Lindbergh Jr., infant son of legendary pilot Charles Lindbergh, is taken from his New Jersey home. Ransom is demanded. A body identified as baby Charles is found two months later.

The Federal Kidnapping Act, also known as the Lindbergh Law, is passed. It allows federal investigation of interstate kidnappings. States follow by passing "Little Lindbergh Laws" related to kidnapping.

1935 Bruno Hauptmann is convicted in the kidnapping of Charles Lindbergh Jr. Ransom money links him to the crime. He is sentenced to die.

1936 Bruno Hauptmann is executed. Many believe he was framed.

1968 The Uniform Child Custody Jurisdiction Act (later revised as the Uniform Child Custody Jurisdiction and Enforcement Act) is passed to help courts in different states cooperate in custody matters.

1974 Nineteen-year-old Patty Hearst, granddaughter of a wealthy newspaper publisher, is kidnapped by a terrorist group. She joins their cause, arguably by force.

1975 The FBI establishes a Missing Person File as part of its NCIC database.

1979 Six-year-old Etan Patz disappears while walking to his school bus stop in New York. The media publicizes the case with the help of photos. Despite remarkable efforts by investigators, Etan remains missing.

A crime spree known as the Atlanta child murders begins; Wayne Williams was later convicted for these crimes in 1982, though some controversy still surrounds the verdict.

1980 The Hague Convention on the Civil Aspects of International Child Abduction promotes the speedy return of children under 16 who are held in a country different from their own.

The Parental Kidnapping Prevention Act is passed to encourage states to honor child custody decisions made in other states and when certain guidelines are met.

1981 Adam Walsh, age six, is kidnapped from a Florida shopping mall and murdered. His parents, John and Revé Walsh, begin their journey as advocates for missing children's causes, and Adam's case brings unprecedented attention to the issue of child abduction.

1982 The Missing Children Act allows information about missing children to be entered into the FBI's National Crime Information Center database.

1983 President Ronald Reagan declares May 25, the anniversary of Etan Patz's disappearance, National Missing Children's Day.

1984 The Missing Children's Assistance Act mandates the creation of a national clearinghouse on missing and exploited children's issues.

The National Center for Missing & Exploited Children opens as the national clearinghouse on missing and exploited children's issues. John and Revé Walsh are co-founders.

1988 NISMART-1 is conducted.

The television show *America's Most Wanted* debuts with John Walsh as its host.

1989 Jacob Wetterling, 11, of Minnesota is seen being kidnapped. He remains missing.

1990 The National Child Search Assistance Act requires that missing child investigations begin without delay.

1993 The International Parental Kidnapping Crime Act strengthens efforts against international kidnapping.

The FBI identifies a serious problem with online predators.

The abduction and murder of 12-year-old Polly Klaas in California stuns the nation.

1994 Seven-year-old Megan Kanka is abducted and murdered by a sex offender in New Jersey.

The Violent Crime Control and Law Enforcement Act passes, which includes the Jacob Wetterling Crimes Against Children and Sexually Violent Offender Registration Act.

1995 The FBI's IINI is launched to fight online sexual exploitation of children.

1996 Amber Hagerman, age nine, is abducted in Texas and murdered. The AMBER Plan, a predecessor to the AMBER Alert, is developed.

Megan's Law is passed nationally, requiring community notification about sex offenders.

1997 Twelve-year-old Laura Smither of Texas is abducted and murdered. Her parents co-found the Laura Recovery Center.

1998 CyberTipline is launched to help people report child sexual exploitation.

Most of NISMART-2 is conducted.

The AMBER Plan leads to the recovery of an infant in Texas.

YISS-1 begins.

2000 Trafficking Victims Protection Act targets traffickers of persons and improves assistance for victims.

Kristen's Act provides federal support for a national clearinghouse for missing adults.

2001 Patty Hearst is pardoned by President Bill Clinton.

2002 The AMBER Alert program is coordinated by the federal government.

Fourteen-year-old Elizabeth Smart is abducted from her home in Utah.

Thirteen-year-old Kacie Woody is abducted and murdered by someone she met online.

2003 The PROTECT Act improves the AMBER Alert and other responses to abduction. It also includes Suzanne's Law, which requires authorities to enter information about missing persons under age 21 into NCIC.

Kidnapping survivor Elizabeth Smart is found on March 12.

2005 YISS-2 is conducted.

2006 The Adam Walsh Child Protection and Safety Act provides for new ways to keep track of sex offenders and protect children.

Endnotes

Introduction

1. U.S. Department of Justice, Office of Justice Programs, "Attorney General Alberto R. Gonzales Marks National Missing Children's Day," http://www.ojp.usd oj.gov/pressreleases/amber 052005.htm.
2. Online Etymology Dictionary, "Abduct," http://www.etymon line.com/index/php?search =abduct&searc hmode=none.
3. Paula S. Fass, *Kidnapped: Child Abduction in America* (Cambridge, Mass.: Harvard University Press, 1997).
4. Ibid.
5. Michael Newton, *The Encyclopedia of Kidnappings* (New York: Checkmark Books, 2002).
6. Ibid.
7. David Finkelhor, Heather Hammer, and Andrea J. Sedlak, *Nonfamily Abducted Children: National Estimates and Characteristics* (Washington, D.C.: Office of Juvenile Justice and Delinquency Prevention, 2002).
8. National Center for Missing & Exploited Children, *Personal Safety for Children: A Guide for Parents.*
9. Crimes Against Children Research Center, "Fact Sheet: Non-Family Abduction," http://www. unh.edu/ccrc/factsheet/nonfam-abduction.htm.

10. Crimes Against Children Research Center, "Fact Sheet: Family Abduction," http://www.unh .edu/ccrc/factsheet/famabdu ction.htm.
11. David Finkelhor and Richard Ormrod, "Kidnapping of Juveniles: Patterns From NIBRS," NCJRS, http://www.ncjrs.gov/ pdffiles1/ojjdp/181161.pdf.
12. Federal Bureau of Investigation, "About Us," http://www.fbi. gov/aboutus/faqs/faqsone.htm.
13. National Center for Missing & Exploited Children, "Federal Statues," http://www.ncmec.org/mi ssingkids/servlet/rg/miss-ingkids/servlet/PageServl et?LanguageCountry=en_ US&PageId=1615.

Chapter 1

1. Fass.
2. National Center for Missing & Exploited Children, "National Missing Children's Day–May 25," http://www.missingkids.com /misskingkids/servlet/Page Servlet?languagecountry= en_US&PageId=1974.
3. Stephen E. Steidel, ed., *Missing and Abducted Children: A Law-Enforcement Guide to Case Investigation and Program Management*, 2d ed. (Alexandria, Va.: National Center for Missing & Exploited Children, 2000).

4. Federal Bureau of Investigation, "Investigative Programs: Crimes Against Children," http://www.fbi.gov/hq/cid/cac/investtext.htm.

5. U.S. Department of Health and Human Services, Administration for Children & Families, "Fact Sheet: Child Victims of Human Trafficking," http://www.acf.hhs.gov/trafficking/about/children_victims.html.

6. "Teen Girls Tell Their Stories of Sex Trafficking and Exploitation in U.S," *ABC News* Internet Ventures, http://www.abcnews.go.com/Primetime/print?id=1596778.

7. U.S. Department of Health & Human Services, "Identifying the Crime of Human Trafficking," http://www.acf.hhs.gov/trafficking/campaign_kits/tool_kit_law/identify_crime.html.

8. U.S. Department of Health & Human Services, Administration for Children & Families, "The Mindset of a Human Trafficking Victim," http://www.acf.hhs.gov/trafficking/campaign_kits/tool_kit_law/mindset_victim.html.

9. ABC News, "Teen Girls Tell Their Stories of Sex Trafficking and Exploitation in U.S.," http://www.abcnews.go.com/Primetime/print?id=1596778.

10. Kathleen Ramsland, "The Polygraph," courtTV Crime Library, http://www.crimelibrary.com/criminal_mind/forensics/polygraph/3.html.

11. Finkelhor, et al., "Kidnapping of Juveniles: Patterns From NIBRS."

12. Jessica Reaves, "How to Keep Your Child Safe," *TIME*, http://www.time.com/time/nation/printout/0,8816,321889,00.html.

13. John Hanna, "Police: Teen's kidnapping story a hoax," http://www.boston.com/news/nation/articles/2006/04/13/police_probe_kan_teens_abduction/.

14. Channel 3000, "Audrey Seiler Sentenced to Probation for Faked Abduction," http://www.channel3000.com/news/3477907/detail.html.

15. Wendy Koch, "Abduction Tale May Be Latest Hoax," *USA TODAY*, December 6, 2006.

Chapter 2

1. Jeff Mosier, "After 10 Years, Anguish over Amber's Abduction Still Fresh," *The Dallas Morning News*, January 13, 2006.

2. U.S. Department of Justice, Office of Justice Programs, "Guidance on Criteria for Issuing AMBER Alerts," http://www.amberalert.gov/docs/AMBERCriteria.pdf.

3. Mosier, "After 10 Years, Anguish over Amber's Abduction Still Fresh."

4. Letter from President George W. Bush to those observing National Missing Children's Day, May 17, 2004.

5. Joann Donnellan, *AMBER Alert* (Alexandria, Va.: National Center for Missing & Exploited Children, 2001).

6. National Center for Missing & Exploited Children, "President Bush Announces Immediate Action to Improve AMBER Alert System," http://www.missing-kids.com/missingkids/servlet/NewsEventServlet?LanguageCountry=en_US&PageId=325.

7. A Child Is Missing, "About Us," http://www.achildismissing.org/default.html?section=about%20us.

8. A Child Is Missing, "A Child Is Missing," http://www.achildismissing.org/default.html?section=home.

9. Donnellan.

10. CNN, "Two Kidnapped California Girls Found Safe," http://cnnstudentnews.cnn.com/TRANSCRIPTS/0208/01/bn.13.html.

11. Jean Guccione, Andrew Blankstein, and Mitchell Landsberg, "Antelope Valley Abductions," *Los Angeles Times*, August 2, 2002.

12. Ian McCann, "Amber Alert Touted," *The Dallas Morning News*, August 4, 2003.

13. National Center for Missing & Exploited Children, "AMBER Alert," http://www.missingkids.com/missingkids/servlet/pageServlet?LanguageCountry=en_US&PageId=991.

14. Donnellan.

15. National Center for Missing & Exploited Children, "AMBER Plan Success Stories 2006," http://www.missingkids.com/missingkids/servlet/PageServlet?LanguageCountry=en_US&PageId=2328.

Chapter 3

1. Kelly, "Kelly," Take Root, http://www.takeroot.org/missing_side/kelly_01.php.

2. "US Department of Justice Statistics on Missing Children," *Action*PACT, Issue 3, November 2003.

3. Heather Hammer, David Finkelhor, and Andrea J. Sedlak, *Children Abducted by Family Members: National Estimates and Characteristics* (Washington, D.C.: Office of Juvenile Justice and Delinquency Prevention, 2002).

4. Hammer.

5. Patricia M. Hoff, *Family Abduction: Prevention and Response* (Alexandria, Va.: National Center for Missing & Exploited Children, 2002).

6. Josh Belzman, "Family Abduction Takes Bitter Toll on Victims," MSNBC, http://www.msnbc.msn.com/id/10038590/print/1/displaymode/1098.

7. Jen, "I've Come Back To You," Take Root, http://takeroot.org/sanctuary/comeback.php.

8. Janet Chiancone, *Parental Abduction: A Review of the Literature* (Washington, D.C.: Office of Juvenile Justice and Delinquency Prevention).

9. *For the Parents* (Washington, D.C.: U.S. Department of State, May 2004).

10. Steidel.

11. U.S. Department of State, "International Child Abduction," http://travel.state.gov/family/abduction/abuction_580.html#.

12. Nancy B. Hammer, "The Myths and Truths of Family Abduction–National Affairs," *USA TODAY* at FindArticles, http: //www.find articles.com/p/articles/mi_m1272/is_2700_132/ai_108 791270.

Chapter 4

1. Lois M. Collins, "Baby Taken from LDS Hospital," *Deseret News*, March 31, 2004.
2. John B. Rabun Jr., *For Healthcare Professionals: Guidelines on Prevention of and Response to Infant Abductions* (Alexandria, Va.: National Center for Missing & Exploited Children, 2005).
3. Ann Wolbert Burgess, and Kenneth V. Lanning, eds., *An Analysis of Infant Abductions* (Alexandria, Va.: National Center for Missing & Exploited Children, 2003).
4. Rabun Jr.
5. Ibid.
6. Burgess.
7. Ibid.
8. Finkelhor.
9. Rabun Jr.
10. Burgess.
11. Larry G. Ankrom and Cynthia J. Lent, "Cradle Robbers: A Study of the Infant Abductor," *The FBI Law Enforcement Bulletin*, September 1995.
12. CBS News, "In-Law Turns In Alleged Baby Snatcher," http: //www.cbsnews.com/stories/2006/09/20/national/main2024771.shtml.
13. Rabun Jr.

Chapter 5

1. *America's Most Wanted*, "The Story of Adam Walsh," http://www.amw.com/fugitives/case.cfm?id=39789.
2. PBS Kids, "Helping Children with Scary News," http://pbskids.org/rogers/parentsteachers/special/scarynews.html.
3. Ernest E. Allen, "Wal-Mart Bank Federal Deposit Insurance Application Public Hearing," National Center for Missing & Exploited Children, http://www.missing-kids.com/missingkids/servlet/NewsEventServlet?LanguageCountry=en_US&PageId=2344.
4. National Center for Missing & Exploited Children, *For Law-Enforcement Professionals*.
5. National Center for Missing & Exploited Children, *re:05, annual report*.
6. National Center for Missing & Exploited Children, "Code Adam," http://www.missingkids.com/missingkids/servlet/serviceServlet?LanguageCountry=en_US&PageId=588.
7. *America's Most Wanted*, "Missing Child Resources," http:// www.amw.com/missingchildren/resources.cfm.
8. Lee McGuire, "Families Mark Missing Children's Day," KVUE News, http://www.kvue.com/news/local/stories/052506kvuemissingchildren-cb.2057ff36.html.
9. RadKIDS, "Polly Klaas Foundation Marks 10th Anniversary of Polly's Abduction with Unprecedented Safety Training

Program," http://www.radkids.org/releases/2003100101/.

10. BeyondMissing, "Marc Klaas," http://www.beyondmissing.com/bio_mk.shtml.

11. Molly M. Ginty, "Grieving Mothers Become Anti-Abduction Crusaders," WeNews, Women's eNews, http://www.womensenews.org/article.cfm/dyn/aid/1924/context/archive.

12. Jessica Marie Lunsford Foundation, "Frequently Asked Questions," http://www.jmlfoundation.com/faq.html.

13. Laura Recovery Center, "Laura Recovery Center," http://: www.lrcf.org/index.html.

14. The Laura Recovery Center Team, *The Laura Recovery Center Manual*, v1.3.5, May 30, 2002.

15. National Center for Missing & Exploited Children, "National Missing Children's Day-May 25," http://www.missingkids.com/missingkids/servlet/PageServlet?LanguageCountry=en_US&PageId=1974.

16. National Center for Missing & Exploited Children, "Picture Them Home," http://www.missingkids.com/missingkids/servlet/CampaignServlet?LanguageCountry=en_US&PageId=259.

17. SmileSafe Kids, "Lifetouch and the National Center for Missing & Exploited Children Partner with Schools across the Country to Launch SmileSafe Kids™," http://schoolportraits.lifetouch.com/uploadedFiles/justForSchools/smilesafe/SmileSafe%20Kids%20news%20release.pdf.

18. ABC News, "Father and Daughter to Be Reunited after 13 Years," http://www.abcnews.go.com/WNT/print?id=1844217.

19. Sue Anne Pressley Montes, "Md. Man Gets to Say, 'Daddy Does Love You,'" *The Washington Post*, April 18, 2006.

20. Department of Justice, Office of Justice Programs, "Attorney General Marks National Missing Children's Day; Presents Awards for Efforts in Missing & Exploited Children Cases," http://www.ojp.usdoj.gov/newsroom/2004/OJP_05192004.htm.

Chapter 6

1. Ed and Lois Smart with Laura Morton, *Bringing Elizabeth Home: A Journey of Faith and Hope* (New York: Doubleday, 2003).

2. CourtTVnews, "Elizabeth Smart's Younger Sister Recounts Abduction Story," http://www.courttv.com/news/2005/0721/sartap.html.

3. Ed Smart.

4. Federal Bureau of Investigation, "Investigative Programs: Crimes Against Children, Kidnapping," http://www.fbi.gov/hq/cid/cac/kidnap.htm.

5. *Recovery and Reunification of Missing Children: A Team Approach* (Alexandria, Va.: National Center for Missing & Exploited Children, 1995).

6. *Missing and Abducted Children: A Law-Enforcement Guide to Case Investigation and Program Management*, 2d ed. (Alexandria, Va.: National Center for Missing & Exploited Children, 2000).

7. Tom Smart and Lee Benson, *In Plain Sight: The Startling Truth Behind the Elizabeth Smart Investigation* (Chicago: Chicago Review Press, 2005).

8. Smart, *Bringing Elizabeth Home: A Journey of Faith and Hope.*

9. Ibid.

10. Ibid.

11. Sean Gregory, "Back From The Blaze," *TIME*, March 15, 2004, http://www.time.com/time/magazine/article/0,9171,993590,00.html.

12. *USA TODAY*, "Mom Takes Home Daughter Thought Killed in 1997 Fire," USATODAY. com, March 9, 2004, http://www.usatoday.com/news/nation/2004-03-09-girl-mom_x.htm.

13. 6abc.com, "Carolyn Correa's Sentencing Day," WPVI-TV/DT Philadelphia, http://abclocal.go.com/wpvistory?section=local&id=3468798.

14. Alissa J. Rubin and Elisabeth Penz, "Young Kidnap Victim Sad, Withdrawn," *Desert Morning News*, http://www.desertnews.com/dn/print/1,1442,645196260,00.html.

15. Rubin.

16. Ibid.

17. *Recovery and Reunification of Missing Children: A Team Approach* (Alexandria, Va.: National Center for Missing & Exploited Children, 1995).

18. Mosier.

19. CourtTVnews, "Judge Declares Man Accused of Kidnapping Elizabeth Smart Unfit for Trial," http://www.courttv.com/news/smart/121806_ap.html.

Chapter 7

1. Wendy Koch, "Kids Run, Shout, Fight—and Foil Abductions," *USA TODAY*, September 6, 2006.

2. WTEN, "Local Hero Receives Courage Award," News 10: WTEN, http://www.wten.com/global/story.asp?s=4951702&ClientType=Printable.

3. National Center for Missing & Exploited Children, "Back-To-School Safety: New NCMEC Analysis Shows More Attempted Abductions Happen During the School Year," http://www.missingkids.org.

4. National Center for Missing & Exploited Children, "National Center for Missing & Exploited Children and Duracell Launch Child Safety Education Campaign for Back-to-School," http://www.missingkids.com/missingkids/servlet/NewsEventServlet?LanguageCountry=en_US&PageId=2773.

5. Janet R. Johnston and Linda K. Girdner, *Family Abductors: Descriptive Profiles and Preventative Interventions, Juvenile Justice Bulletin* (Washington, D.C.: U.S. Department of Jus-

tice, Office of Justice Programs, Office of Juvenile Justice and Delinquency Prevention, January 2001).

6. Johnston, et al.

7. National Center for Missing & Exploited Children, *Just in Case...Guidelines in case you are considering family separation* (Alexandria, Va.: National Center for Missing & Exploited Children, 2005).

8. Gavin De Becker, *Protecting the Gift: Keeping Children and Teenagers Safe (and Parents Sane)* (New York: Random House, 1999).

9. CBS NEWS, "College Kids Easy Prey For Abductors," CBSNews.com, September 27, 2006, http://www.cbsnews.com/stories/2006/09/27/earlyshow/printable2042235.shtml.

10. BobStuber.com, "Back to School Safety Tips," http://www.bobstuber.com/back2school.htm.

11. BobStuber.com, "Tips to Avoid Abduction," http://www.bobstuber.com/abduction.htm.

12. ABC News, "How Abductors Get Willing Victims," http://www.abcnews.go.com/Primetime/print?id=590415.

Chapter 8

1. Federal Bureau of Investigation, "Headline Archives: 10 Years of Protecting Our Children," http://www.fbi.gov/page2/dec03/online120203.htm.

2. Federal Bureau of Investigation, "Headline Archives: Innocent Images," http://www.fbi.gov/page2/feb06/innocentimages10years2.htm.

3. Federal Bureau of Investigation, "Headline Archives: 10 Years of Protecting Our Children," http://www.fbi.gov.

4. Federal Bureau of Investigation, "Innocent Images National Initiative," http://www.fbi.gov/publications/innocent.htm.

5. Federal Bureau of Investigation, "Innocent Images National Initiative," http://www.fbi.gov.

6. Federal Bureau of Investigation, "Investigative Programs: Crimes Against Children," http://www.fbi.gov/hq/cid/cac/investtext.htm.

7. U.S. Department of Justice, "Project Safe Childhood," Project Safe Childhood, http://www.projectsafechildhood.gov/guide.htm.

8. *A Parent's Guide to Internet Safety* (Calverton, Md.: Federal Bureau of Investigation, Cyber Division, 2000).

9. Associated Press, "Chat Rooms Help FBI Hunt for Pedophiles," MSNBC, http://www.msnbc.msn.com/id/12796965/.

10. "Deputy Assistant Attorney General Daley Addresses 'Bringing Our Missing Children Home Safely' Conference," *OJJDP NEWS @ a Glance*, November/December 2006.

11. National Center for Missing & Exploited Children, "CyberTipline Success Stories," http://us.missingkids.com/missingkids/servlet/PageServlet?LanguageCountry=en_US&PageId=376.

12. Janis Wolak, Kimberly Mitchell, and David Finkelhor of the Crimes Against Children Research Center, University of New Hampshire, *Online Victimization of Youth: Five Years Later* (Alexandria, Va.: National Center for Missing & Exploited Children, 2006).

13. Lawrence J. Magid, *Teen Safety on the Information Highway* (Alexandria, Va.: National Center for Missing & Exploited Children, 2003).

14. Cathy Frye, "Caught in the Web," American Society of Newspaper Editors, http:// www.asne.org/print.cfm?printer_page=%2Findex.cfm%3FID%3D5588.

15. Family Life Today, "Kacie Woody's Story," FamilyLife, http://www.familylife.com/fltoday/default.asp?id=7633.

16. Federal Bureau of Investigation, Little Rock, "Press Release," http://littlerock.fbi.gov/pressrel/2004/press10120 4.htm.

17. Frye.

18. Kacie Woody Foundation, "All About Us," http://home.alltel.net/rkw/about_us.htm.

19. Magid.

Chapter 9

1. New York State Division of State Police, "Missing: Suzanne G. Lyall," http://www.troopers.state.ny.us/Wanted_and_Missing/Missing/Viewcfm?ID=7D2586B3-87FC-44BB-B602-52825C71E4F0.

2. Lara Jakes, "Lyalls on hand for signing of safety bill," *Times Union*, April 7, 1999.

3. Douglas Lyall and Mary Lyall, "Lyalls Seek Changes to Help Families with Missing Children," Help us find Suzanne, http://www.global2000.net/suzy/changes.html.

4. National Center for Missing Adults, *The Missing Voice* (Phoenix, Ariz.: National Center for Missing Adults, July 2006).

5. David Krajicek, "America's Missing," CourtTV Crime Library, http://www.crimelibrary.com/criminal_mind/forensics/americas_missing/2.html.

6. U.S. Department of Justice, Office of Justice Programs, "Incident-Based Statistics," http://www.ojp.usdoj.gov/bjs/ibrs.htm.

7. CNN, "'Runaway Bride' on the Rebound," CNN.com, May 19, 2006, http://www.cnn.com/2006/US/05/19/runaway.bride/index. html.

8. CBS News, "'Runaway Bride' Sues Ex for $500,000," http://www.cbsnews.com/stories/2006/10/10/national/main2076613.shtml?CMP=ILC-SearchStories.

9. *USA TODAY*, "Parents Charged with Abducting Bride," USA-TODAY.com, October 3, 2006, http://www.usatoday.com/news/nation/2006-10-03-kidnapped-bride_x.htm.

10. Michael Newton, *The Encyclopedia of Kidnappings* (New York: Checkmark Books, 2002).

11. Team HOPE, "Missing Adult Children," http://www.teamhope.org/adultsdo.html.

12. Lewis Kamb, "Missing Persons," *The IRE Journal*, July/August 2003 at Find Articles, http://findarticles.com/p/articles/mi_qa3720/is_200307/ai_n9250393/print.

13. Office of the Attorney General, Washington State, "Task Force to Aid in Missing-Person Investigations," http://www.atg.wa.gov/releases/rel_missing_121704.html.

14. Office of the Attorney General, Washington State, "Your Loved One Is Missing!!!," http://www.atg.wa.gov/law/documents/Missing_Persons_11_2004.pdf.

Glossary

abduct   To take away or detain a person wrongfully.

ACIM   A Child Is Missing, a telephone alert system that encourages the public to help when a young, elderly, or disabled person is missing.

AMBER Alert   America's Missing: Broadcast Emergency Response Alert, which tells the public about particularly serious missing children cases that meet certain guidelines.

brainwashed   Forcefully influenced to think or believe differently than one normally would.

CARD   Child Abduction Rapid Deployment, an FBI program that sends expert teams to help with abduction investigations.

CART   Child Abduction Response Team program, which is supported by the U.S. Department of Justice and complements the AMBER Alert system regionally.

child   A person who has not reached a certain age, usually 18.

custody   Responsibility for a child's care.

CyberTipline   A tool for reporting child sexual exploitation; call 1-800-843-5678 or visit cybertipline.com.

DNA   Deoxyribonucleic acid, which carries genetic information and helps to identify people.

family abduction   The kidnapping of a child by a relative or someone who represents a relative.

FBI   Federal Bureau of Investigation; the main investigative arm of the United States Department of Justice.

federal   Of or related to the central government rather than its individual states.

felony   A most serious crime.

forensic   Pertaining to legal issues.

forensic imaging   The use of images, such as photos and videos, as they relate to legal issues.

frame   To make an innocent person appear guilty.

human trafficking   Modern-day slavery that involves forcing or tricking victims.

ICAC   Internet Crimes Against Children Task Force program, funded by the U.S. Department of Justice to target online dangers, educate communities, and help victims.

IINI   Innocent Images National Initiative, an FBI effort to stop online exploitation of children.

infant abduction   The abduction of a baby six months old or younger by someone outside its family.

instinct   A natural impulse.

international abduction   A family abduction in which the victim is taken to or retained in another country wrongfully.

kidnap   To take away or detain a person wrongfully.

Kristen's Law   A law that established federal support for a national clearinghouse for missing adults.

left-behind parent   The parent from whom a child has been abducted.

Lindbergh Law   The Federal Kidnapping Act of 1932, which allowed federal investigation of suspected interstate kidnappings.

lure   To trick or entice a person, especially a child, into an unsafe situation.

media   Means of communicating with the public, such as television stations, newspapers, radio stations, and magazines.

Megan's Law   A law that provides for community notification about sex offenders.

misdemeanor   A less serious crime in comparison to a felony.

NCIC   The FBI's National Crime Information Center database, which includes missing person records.

NCMA   National Center for Missing Adults, a national clearinghouse that helps with missing adult issues.

NCMEC   National Center for Missing & Exploited Children, a national clearinghouse that provides services related to abducted, endangered, and sexually exploited children.

NISMART-2   Second National Incidence Studies of Missing, Abducted, Runaway, and Thrownaway Children.

nonfamily abduction   An abduction in which the perpetrator is not in the victim's family.

pedophile   An adult who is sexually interested in young children.

perpetrator   A person responsible for wrongdoing.

polygraph   An instrument that evaluates deception.

predator   Someone who hunts for people to victimize.

profile   A description of what a person might be like.

prosecute   To proceed with legal action against someone in court.

register   Officially provide.

ransom   Money or other payment demanded or given in exchange for a victim.

reunification   The return of a victim to his or her family.

sex offender   Someone convicted of a sex crime.

state missing children's clearinghouse   A state organization that helps with missing children cases.

stereotypical kidnapping   Rare kind of abduction in which the perpetrator is a stranger or slight acquaintance and particular factors are involved.

Stockholm syndrome   A psychological reaction in which the victim identifies with the captor, perhaps as a way to survive.

Suzanne's Law   A law that requires the entry of missing persons under age 21 into the FBI's NCIC database.

Team HOPE   A group that supports and empathizes with families of missing children.

victim   A person who has been harmed.

Youth Internet Safety Surveys   Research that evaluates children's online safety.

Bibliography

2 SMRT 4U. "SMRT Tips." http://www.2smrt4u.com/tips.html.

A Child Is Missing. "Sherry Friedlander-Olsen Founder." http://www.achildismissing.org/frMain.lasso?section=about%20us&id=699.

Allen, Ernie. *"The Kid Is With a Parent, How Bad Can It Be?": The Crisis of Family Abductions.* Alexandria, Va.: National Center for Missing & Exploited Children, 1991.

————. "Sexual Exploitation of Children over the Internet: What Parents, Kids and Congress Need to Know about Child Predators." National Center for Missing & Exploited Children. http://www.missing-kids.com/missingkids/servlet/NewsEventServlet?LanguageCountry=en_US&PageId=2345.

"AMBER Alert History," *The Dallas Morning News*, January 13, 2006.

AMBER Alert, Utah Broadcasters Association.

American Polygraph Association. "Frequently Asked Questions." http://www.polygraph.org/Press/FAQ.htm.

Anhalt, Karen Nickel. "Kidnapped Girl Wondered, 'Why Me?'" *People Weekly.* http://people.aol.com/people/article/0, 26334,1532268,00.html.

Barron, James. "Vigil for Slain Girl, 7, Backs a Law on Offenders." *The New York Times,* August 3, 1994.

BBC On This Day. "1974: Newspaper Heiress Kidnapped." BBC NEWS. http://news.bbc.co.uk/onthisday/hi/dates/stories/february/5/newsid_2867000/2867727.stm.

Biography Resource Center. "Patty Hearst." Gale Group. http://galenet.galegroup.com/servlet/BioRC.

Blog Beware. Alexandria, Va.: National Center for Missing & Exploited Children, 2006.

Brown, Steven Kerry. *The Complete Idiot's Guide to Private Investigating.* Indianapolis: Alpha Books, 2003.

"California AMBER ALERT-Summary Information." California Highway Patrol. http://www.chp.ca.gov/amber/amb_summaries.html.

Carole Sund/Carrington Memorial Reward Foundation. "The Sund-Pelosso Story." http://www.carolesundfoundation.com/sections/about.

CBS NEWS. "Keys to Protecting Kids Online? Talk!" CBS.com. http://www.cbsnews.com/stories/2006/04/05/earlyshow/living/parenting/main1473951.shtml.

Chang, Andrew. "R-JENERATION: Who's Talking?" http://www.review journal.com/lvrj_hohome/2004/Feb-17-Tue-2004/living/2306 7556.html.

Child Lures Prevention. "Child Internet Safety Tips." http://www.child luresprevention.com/parents/internet_safety.asp.

Clark, John C. "Runaway Bride Sues Ex-Fiance for $500K." ABC News. http://abcnews.go.com/US/wireStory?id=2550874.

CNN. "DNA Confirms Identity of Kidnapped Austrian Girl." http://www.cnn.com/2006/WORLD/europe/08/25/austria.kidnap/index.html.

CNN. "Jurors: Megan Kanka's Killer Should Die." http://www.cnn.com/US/9706/20/kanka.verdict/index.html?eref=sitesearch.

CNN. "Parents Can Teach Kids to Stop Abductions." http://www.cnn.com/2004/US/02/05/child.safety.tips/index.html.

CNN. "Tearful Bride Testifies against Her Parents." http://www.cnn.com/2006/LAW/12/07/kidnapped.bride.ap/index.html.

CNN. "Woman Pleads Not Guilty to Snatching Baby Abby," http://www.cnn.com/2006/LAW/09/21/baby.missing/index.html.

Court TV Library. "New Jersey v. Timmendequas (5/97)." http://www.courttv.com/archive/casefiles/verdicts/kanka.html.

Court TV News. "'Runaway Bride' Jennifer Wilbanks Sues Former Fiancé for $500,000." http://www.courttv.com/people/2006/1010/jennifer_wilbanks_ap.html.

Daniels, Deborah J. *Remarks of the Honorable Deborah J. Daniels, Assistant Attorney General, Office of Justice Programs, at the Department of Justice National Missing Children's Day Ceremony*, May 19, 2004.

Department of Justice, Office of Justice Programs. "Attorney General Alberto R. Gonzales Marks National Missing Children's Day." http://www.ojp.usdoj.gov/newsroom/2006/DOJ06-326.htm.

Department of Justice, Office of Justice Programs. "Department of Justice Holds First Training Session on Child Abduction Response Teams." http://www.ojp.gov/newsroom/2006/OJJDP06033.htm.

Dickinson, Amy. "The New Safety Rules for Kids." *TIME*, July 29, 2002.

Duracell, and National Center for Missing & Exploited Children. "Child Safety Toolkit." http://www.duracell.com/us/parents.

Fact Sheet: Child Abduction Response Teams (CART). Washington, D.C.: U.S. Department of Justice, Office of Justice Programs, 2006.

FamilyLife Today. "Kacie Woody's Story." http://www.familylife.com/fltoday/default.asp?id=7633.

Federal Bureau of Investigation. "CARD." http://www.fbi.gov/card.

Federal Bureau of Investigation. "Famous Cases: The Lindbergh Kidnapping." http://www.fbi.gov/libref/historic/famcases/lindber/lindbernew.htm.

Federal Bureau of Investigation. "Headline Archives: Keeping Kids Safe Online." http://www.fbi.gov/page2/april06/ccctf_interview.042806.htm.

Federal Bureau of Investigation. "Headline Archives: When Kids Go Missing." http://www.fbi.gov/page2/june06/card_teams061606.htm.

Federal Bureau of Investigation. "Investigative Programs, Crimes against Children, Investigating Crimes against Children." http://www.fbi.gov/hq/cid/cac/investtext.htm.

Federal Bureau of Investigation. "Investigative Programs, Crimes against Children, Kidnappings." http://www.fbi.gov/hq/cid/cac/kidnap.htm.

Federal Bureau of Investigation. "NCIC Missing Person and Unidentified Person Statistics for 2005." http://www.fbi.gov/hq/cjisd/missingpersons.htm.

Federal Bureau of Investigation. "A Parent's Guide to Internet Safety." http://www.fbi.gov/publications/pguide/pguidee.htm.

Federal Bureau of Investigation. "Safety Tips: Child Abduction." http://www.fbi.gov/kids/k5th/safety3.htm.

Federal Bureau of Investigation. "Safety Tips: Internet Safety." http://www.fbi.gov/kids/k5th/safety2.htm.

Federal Trade Commission. *Social Networking Sites: Safety Tips for Tweens and Teens*. Washington, D.C.: Federal Trade Commission, May 2006.

Fields-Meyer, Thomas, and Maureen Harrington. "Safe Passage." *People Weekly*, April 5, 2004.

Finkelhor, David, Heather Hammer, and Andrea J. Sedlak. *Nonfamily Abducted Children: National Estimates and Characteristics*. Washington, D.C.: Office of Juvenile Justice and Delinquency Prevention, 2002.

Fodor, Margie Druss. *Megan's Law: Protection or Privacy*. Berkeley Heights, N.J.: Enslow Publishers, 2001.

FOX News.com. "Coed Who Faked Abduction Gets Probation." http://www.foxnews.com/story/0,2933,124413,00.html.

FOXNews.com. "Missouri Woman Pleads Not Guilty to Kidnapping Baby, Attacking Mom." http://www.foxnews.com/story/0,2933,214999,00.html.

Gado, Mark. "My Baby Is Missing!" http://www.crimelibrary.com/criminal_mind/psychology/child_abduction/.

Garcia, Eric. "Girl abducted in Arlington." *The Dallas Morning News*, January 14, 1996.

Girls' Life. "Escape artist." http://www.findarticles.com/p/articles/mi_
m0IBX/is_3_12/ai_n15881138.

Gordon, Glenn. "Increase Your Child's Chance of Staying Safe." *Los
Angeles Family Magazine.* http://www.lafamily.com/display_article
.php?id=992.

Grolier Multimedia Encyclopedia. "Hearst, Patricia." http://gme.grolier
.com/cgi-bin/article?assetid=0134445-0.

Haberman, Maggie, and Jeane MacIntosh. *Held Captive: The Kidnapping and Rescue of Elizabeth Smart.* New York: Avon Books,
2003.

Hammer, Heather, David Finkelhor, and Andrea J. Sedlak. *Children
Abducted by Family Members: National Estimates and Characteristics.* Washington, D.C.: Office of Juvenile Justice and Delinquency Prevention, 2002.

Hayes, Ashley. "Utah Girl to Receive Award for Fighting Off Kidnapper." http://www.ksl.com/index.php?nid=148&sid=277747.

Hoff, Patricia M. *The Uniform Child-Custody Jurisdiction and Enforcement Act.* Washington, D.C.: U.S. Department of Justice, Office of
Justice Programs, Office of Juvenile Justice and Delinquency Prevention, December 2001.

Hughes, Donna M. *Hiding in Plain Sight.* Washington, D.C.: U.S.
Department of Health & Human Services, Administration for Children & Families, 2003.

ICAC Task Force. "About Us." http://www.icactraining.org/about. htm.

Independence Hall Association. "The Story of Charley Ross." http://
www.ushistory.org/germantown/upper/charley.htm.

Investigative Checklist for First Responders. Alexandria, Va.: National
Center for Missing & Exploited Children.

Israelsen, Sara. "Parents Charged with Kidnapping Daughter." http:
//www.findarticles.com/p/articles/mi_qn4188/is_20060930
/ai_n16762189.

Jerome, Richard, Maria Eftimades, Nick Gallo, and Stephen Sawicki.
"Megan's legacy." *People Weekly,* March 20, 1995.

Johnson, Kevin. "Budget Woes Wear on Center for Missing Adults."
USA TODAY, November 3, 2006.

The Joyful Child Foundation. "Frequently Asked Questions." http://
www.thejoyfulchild.org/FAQ.html.

Juvenile Justice Digest. "Washington Develops Missing Person Rules."
http://findarticles.com/p/articles/mi_qa3985/is_200401/ai_
n9403463/print.

Kacie Woody Foundation. "Kacie Renè Woody." http://home.alltel.
net/rkw/kaciewoody_a.html.

Kacie Woody Foundation. "Kacie Woody Foundation." http://home.
alltel.net/rkw/kacie.htm.

Kamb, Lewis. "Without a Trace, Part 10: Experts List Ways to Improve System." http://seattlepi.newsource.com/local/110245_fixmissing 27.shtml.

"Kidnapping." http://www.encyclopedia.com/ html/k/kidnappi.asp.

Klaas Kids Foundation. "About the Klaas Kids Foundation For Children." http://www.klaaskids.org/pg-prog.htm.

Klaas Kids Foundation. "Child Safety." http://www.klaaskids.org/pg_cs_childsafety.htm.

KlaasKids Foundation. "Our Story." http://www.klaaskids.org/pgourstory.htm.

Know the Rules. Alexandria, Va.: National Center for Missing & Exploited Children, 2004.

Know the Rules...Abduction and Kidnapping Prevention Tips for Parents and Guardians. Alexandria, Va.: National Center for Missing & Exploited Children, 2002.

Know the Rules: After-School Safety for Children Who Are Home Alone. Alexandria, Va.: National Center for Missing & Exploited Children, 2000.

Know the Rules: Just in Case You... Alexandria, Va.: National Center for Missing Exploited Children, 2002.

Know the Rules...School Safety Tips. Alexandria, Va.: National Center for Missing & Exploited Children, 1994.

The Kristen Foundation. "About Us." http://www.kristenfoundation. org/cgi-bin/datacgi/database.cgi?file=hw&report=spt=sp&ID=001.

Laura Recovery Center, *Annual Report 2005*.

Laura Recovery Center. "Our Background." http://www.lrcf.org/background.html.

Leonard, Christopher. "Hearing for accused baby kidnapper delayed." http://www.stltoday.com/stltoday/news/stories.nsf/mis souristatenews/story/D1088B158360BC5E8625724B0078B482?Op enDocument&highlight=2%2C%22ochsenbine%22.

Lord, Wayne D. "Investigating Potential Child Abduction Cases: A Developmental Perspective." *The FBI Law Enforcement Bulletin*, April 2001.

Lynch, Richard. *Private Investigator's Guide for the Investigation and Location of Missing and Abducted Children*. Austin, Tex.: Thomas Investigative Publications, 1996.

Magid, Lawrence J. *Child Safety on the Information Highway*. Alexandria, Va.: National Center for Missing & Exploited Children, 2005.

———. "Protect Kids on MySpace." http://www.cbsnews.com/stories/ 2006/02/03/scitech/pcanswer/printable1277909.shtml.

Mayo Clinic. "Teaching Skills, Instilling Confidence Best Ways to Prevent Child Abduction." http://www.mayoclinic.org/news2004-rst /2452.html.

McBride, Nancy. "Child Safety Is More than a Slogan." http: //www.mis
    singkids.com/missingkids/servlet/ResourceServlet?LanguageCoun
    try=en_US&PageId=2050.
McGraw, Seamus. "All about Megan's Law." http://www.crimelibrary.
    com/serial_killers/predators/kanka/1.html.
Medaris, Michael, and Cathy Girouard. *Protecting Children in Cyber-
    space: The ICAC Task Force Program.* Washington, D.C.: U.S.
    Department of Justice, Office of Justice Programs, Office of Juve-
    nile Justice and Delinquency Prevention, 2002.
"Missing Independence Girl Found Safe." http://www.ksn.com/news/
    local/3841366.html.
Montaldo, Charles. "Teen Reports Kidnapping to Police." About:
    Crime/Punishment. http://crime.about.com/od/current/a/kelsey_
    call.htm.
Moore, Linda K. "Amber Alert Program Technology." http://digital
    .library.unt.edu/govdocs/crs/peovdocs/crs/permalink/meta-crs-
    7629.tkl.
The Morning Call. "How to Prevent Your Child Getting Abducted."
    http://www.mcall.com/features/family/familyproject/all-5713919
    sep16,0,3651799.story.
MSNBC. "Girl Fights Off Abductor." http://www.msnbc.msn.com/id/
    8799751.
National Center for Missing Adults. "About NMCO." http://www.
    theyaremissed.org/ncma/content.php?webid=about_nmco.
National Center for Missing Adults. "About Our Agency (NCMA)."
    http://www.theyaremissed.org/ncma/content.php?webid=about_
    ncma.
National Center for Missing Adults. "Kristen's Law." http://www.
    theyaremissed.org/ncma/content.php?webid=kristens_law.
National Center for Missing Adults. "Missing Persons Gallery – Endan-
    gered Missing Adult: Kristen Deborah Modafferi." http://www
    .theyaremissed.org/ncma/gallery/ncmaprofile_all_print.php?
    A200300325W.
National Center for Missing Adults. "National Center for Miss-
    ing Adults May Close Doors." http://www.theyaremiss ed.org/
    ncma/10-23-2006.pdf.
National Center for Missing & Exploited Children. "2006 National
    Missing and Exploited Children's Awards." http://www.missing
    kids.com/missingkids/servlet/PageServlet?LanguageCountry=en_
    US&PageId=2378.
National Center for Missing & Exploited Children. "ADT- Sponsored
    Code Adam Program Helps Reunite Parents with Lost Children
    During Hectic Holiday Shopping Season." http://www.missing

kids.com/missingkids/servlet/NewsEventServlet?LanguageCountry=en_US&PageId=2220.

National Center for Missing & Exploited Children. "Amber Hagerman." http://www.ncmec.org/missingkids/servlet/pageServlet?LanguageCountry=en_US&PageId=2242.

National Center for Missing & Exploited Children. "Federal Statutes." http://www.ncmec.org/missingkids/servlet/pageServlet?LanguageCountry=en_US&PageId=1615.

National Center for Missing & Exploited Children. "Frequently Asked Questions." http://www.missingkids.com/en_US/documents/Presskit_FAQ.pdf.

National Center for Missing & Exploited Children. "Frequently Asked Questions and Statistics." http://www. missingkids.com/missingkids/servlet/PageServlet?LanguageCountry=en_US&PageId=242.

National Center for Missing & Exploited Children. *Guidelines for Programs to Reduce Child Victimization: A Resource for Communities When Choosing a Program to Teach Personal Safety to Children.* Alexandria, Va.: National Center for Missing & Exploited Children, 1999.

National Center for Missing & Exploited Children. "The Importance of Having a Good Photo of Your Child." http://www.missingkids.com/missingkids/servlet/PageServlet?LanguageCountry=en_US&PageId=2356.

National Center for Missing & Exploited Children. "National Mandate and Mission." http://www.ncmec.org/missingkids/servlet/PageServlet?LanguageCountry=en_US&PageId=1866.

National Center for Missing & Exploited Children, "President Bush Signs Landmark Sex Offender and Child Protection Legislation on 25th Anniversary of Adam Walsh's Abduction." http://www.missingkids.com/missingkids/servlet/NewsEventServlet?LanguageCountry=en_US&PageId=2503.

The New York Times. "AROUND THE NATION; Miss Hearst's Kidnapper Is Freed on Parole." http://query.nytimes. com/gst/fullpage.html?res=9900E6D61238F935A35756C0A965948260.

Office of Juvenile Justice and Delinquency Prevention. "AMBER Alert: Bringing Abducted Children Home." http://www.ncjrs.gov/html/ojjdp/amberalert/000712/index.html.

Office of Juvenile Justice and Delinquency Prevention. "Attorney General Appoints AAG Daniels National Coordinator for AMBER Alert." http://www.ncjrs.gov/html/ojjdp/news_at_glance/2002_11_6/special_feature.html.

O'Hara, Charles E. and Gregory L. O'Hara. *Fundamentals of Criminal Investigation.* 6th ed. Springfield, Ill.: Charles C. Thomas, 1994.

Oleksyn, Veronika. "Austrian Woman Says She Was Held Captive for Eight Years," *USA TODAY*, August 25, 2006.

The Oprah Winfrey Show. "Back to School Reminders." http://www.oprah.com/tows/pastshows/tows_2000/tows_past_20000831_b.jhtml.

The Oprah Winfrey Show. "Prevent Your Child from Being Abducted." http://www.oprah.com/tows/pastshows/tows_2002/tows_past_20020919_c.jhtml.

Park Alumni Society. "Kristen's Story." http://www.parkscholars.org/garden/kristen.php.

Pasqualini, Kym L. "Kym's Blog." http://while-here.blogspot.com.

Personal communication with Rick Woody. January 9, 2007.

Personal Safety for Children: A Guide for Parents. Alexandria, Va.: National Center for Missing & Exploited Children, 1998.

Please Help Find Our Daughter, Kristen. "Kristen's Law…" http://www.modlink.com/kristen/html/kristenslaw.htm.

Please Help Find Our Daughter, Kristen. "The Search for Kristen…" http://www.modlink.com/kristen/html/search. htm.

"Police Shootout Kills Kidnapper; California Girls Rescued." *Jet*, August 19, 2002.

Polly Klaas Foundation. "FAQs." http://www.pollyklaas.org/about/faq.html.

Polly Klaas Foundation. "Polly Klaas Foundation History." http://www.pollyklaas.org/about/history.html.

Ramsland, Katherine. "The Claiming of Patty Hearst." http://www.crimelibrary.com/terrorists_spies/terrorists/hearst/1.html.

———. "Literary Forensics." http://www.crimelibrary.com/forensics/literary/.

Ritter, Nancy. "Digital Evidence: How Law Enforcement Can Level the Playing Field With Criminals." *National Institute of Justice JOURNAL*, July 2006.

Sedlak, Andrea J., David Finkelhor, Heather Hammer, and Dana J. Schultz. *National Estimates of Missing Children: An Overview*. Washington, D.C.: Office of Juvenile Justice and Delinquency Prevention, 2002.

Simons, Andre B. "Runaway or Abduction? – Brief Article." *The FBI Law Enforcement Bulletin*, November 2000.

Smart, Tom, and Lee Benson. *In Plain Sight: The Startling Truth Behind the Elizabeth Smart Investigation*. Chicago: Chicago Review Press, 2005.

Smith, Thomas B., Kenneth Buniak, Lee Condon, and Lee Reed. *Children Missing from Care: The Law-Enforcement Response*. Alexandria, Va.: National Center for Missing & Exploited Children, 2005.

Snyder, Howard N., and Melissa Sickmund. *Juvenile Offenders and Victims: 2006 National Report.* Washington, D.C.: U.S. Department of Justice, Office of Justice Programs, Office of Juvenile Justice and Delinquency Prevention.

Swanson, Charles R., Neil C. Chamelin, and Leonard Territo. *Criminal Investigation.* 8th ed. New York: McGraw-Hill, 2003.

Swanson, Charles R., Neil C. Chamelin, Leonard Territo, and Robert W. Taylor. *Criminal Investigation.* 9th ed. New York: McGraw-Hill, 2006.

Team HOPE. "The Law." http://www.teamhope.org/law.html.

Team HOPE. "Resources for Missing Adult Children." http://www.teamhope.org/adultsresources.html.

Thomson, Linda. "10 Years to Life for Girl's Kidnapping." http://www.msnbc.msn.com/id/87 99751.

The Tyra Banks Show. "Web of Lies: Online Sex Crimes Exposed." http://tyrashow.warnerbros.com/show_recaps/show_recap_wed53.html.

United States Postal Service. "AMBER Alert." http://shop.usps.com/webapp/wcs/stores/servlet/ProductDisplay?catalogId=101 52&storeId=10001&categoryId=11834&productId=22503&langId=-1.

U.S. Department of Health & Human Services, Administration for Children & Families. "About Human Trafficking." http://www.acf.hhs.gov/trafficking/about/index.html.

U.S. Department of Justice, Office of Justice Programs. "Frequently Asked Questions on AMBER Alert." http://www.amberalert.gov/faqs.html.

U.S. Department of Justice, Office of Justice Programs. "Remarks of Cybele K. Daley, Deputy Assistant Attorney General, Office of Justice Programs at the Child Abduction Response Team Training on Thursday, January 26, 2006, San Diego, CA." http://www.ojp.usdoj.gov/aag/ speeches/CART.htm.

Wal-Mart Good Works. "Code Adam." http://www.walmartfoundation.org/wmstore/goodworks/scripts/Children.jsp?oid=-10261&coid=-10271.

The White House. "Fact Sheet: The Adam Walsh Child Protection And Safety Act of 2006." http://www.whitehouse.gov/news/releases/2006/07/print/20060727-7.html.

Wills, Todd. "Tragedy spurred Amber Plan creation." *The Dallas Morning News*, November 28, 1999.

WNDU-TV. "Taking effective steps to protect our children." http://www.wndu.com/news/092006/news_52548.php.

Wooden, Ken. *Think First & Stay Safe!™ Parent Guide.* Shelburne, Vt.: Child Lures Ltd., 2006.

Woodhouse, Jennifer. "Four safety rules every kid must know." *Redbook*, December 2002.

Wrightsman, Lawrence S., Edie Greene, Michael T. Nietzel and William H. Fortune. *Psychology and the Legal System:* 5th ed. Belmont, Calif.: Wadsworth Group, 2002.

Further Resources

Books

Balcavage, Dynise. *The Federal Bureau of Investigation*. Philadelphia: Chelsea House Publishers, 2000.

Denenberg, Barry. *An American Hero: The True Story of Charles A. Lindbergh*. New York: Scholastic, 1996.

Fodor, Margie Druss. *Megan's Law: Protection or Privacy*. Berkeley Heights, N.J.: Enslow Publishers, 2001.

DVDs

Internet Safety (DVD)
The Safe Side LLC, 2006
Promotes online safety and features John Walsh.

KidSmartz: Abduction Prevention (DVD)
Showtime Networks Inc., 2003
Offers prevention tips for parents and children.

Tricky People (DVD)
Yello Dyno, 1998
Provides safety information for children.

Web Sites

2 SMRT 4U
http://www.2smrt4u.com
Teaches about online safety.

A Child Is Missing
http://www.achildismissing.org
Describes the A Child Is Missing alert program.

AMBER Alert
http://www.amberalert.gov
Provides information related to the AMBER Alert.

Association of Missing and Exploited Children's Organizations
http://www.amecoinc.org
Promotes high-quality services for missing and exploited children and their families.

BeyondMissing
http://www.beyondmissing.com
Helps with creation and distribution of missing child flyers.

The Carole Sund/Carrington Memorial Reward Foundation
http://www.carolesundfoundation.com
Posts rewards in missing person investigations.

Child Lures Prevention
http://www.childlures.com
Educates about personal safety, including common lures.

CyberTipline
http://www.cybertipline.com
Allows reporting of child sexual exploitation.

Don't Believe the Type
http://tcs.cybertipline.com
Informs about Internet dangers.

Federal Bureau of Investigation (Kids' Page)
http://www.fbi.gov/fbikids.htm
Covers investigation, safety, and other kids' topics.

Jacob Wetterling Foundation
http://www.jwf.org
Uses education to prevent exploitation of children.

The Jessica Marie Lunsford Foundation
http://www.jmlfoundation.org
Assists children in crisis through legislation and other means.

The Joyful Child Foundation
http://thejoyfulchild.org
Protects children through programs that support communities.

Kacie Woody Foundation
http://kaciewoody.homestead.com

Shares information about Internet safety and predators.

KlaasKids Foundation
http://www.klaaskids.org
Aims to stop crimes against children.

The Kristen Foundation
http://www.kristenfoundation.org
Works to reunite families with missing people.

Laura Recovery Center
http://www.lrcf.org
Helps with search and prevention efforts.

National Center for Missing Adults
http://www.theyaremissed.org
Provides national services related to missing adults.

National Center for Missing & Exploited Children
http://www.missingkids.com
*Serves as a national clearinghouse on missing and exploited children
    issues.*

NetSmartz Workshop
http://www.netsmartz.org
Educates families and professionals about Internet concerns.

Polly Klaas Foundation
http://www.pollyklaas.org
Addresses missing children issues.

Take Root
http://www.takeroot.org
Empowers former abducted children.

Team HOPE
http://www.teamhope.org
*Supports families of missing children with volunteers who
    understand.*

Wireless AMBER Alerts™ System
https://www.wirelessamberalerts.org/index.jsp
Simplifies signing up for free wireless AMBER Alerts.

Index

Page numbers in *italics* indicate images.

About the Author

Susan O'Brien is a writer who specializes in children's issues. She has an M.A. in forensic psychology and has worked with a variety of organizations, including *USA TODAY* and *PI Magazine*. She was also a registered private investigator in Virginia. Her next writing project is a mystery about a missing person.

The author donates a portion of her earnings from Child Abduction and Kidnapping *to the National Center for Missing & Exploited Children.*

About the
Consulting Editor

John L. French is a 31-year veteran of the Baltimore City Police Crime Laboratory. He is currently a crime laboratory supervisor. His responsibilities include responding to crime scenes, overseeing the preservation and collection of evidence, and training crime scene technicians. He has been actively involved in writing the operating procedures and technical manual for his unit and has conducted training in numerous areas of crime scene investigation. In addition to his crime scene work, Mr. French is also a published author, specializing in crime fiction. His short stories have appeared in *Alfred Hitchcock's Mystery Magazine* and numerous anthologies.